# Principals of Contract Law

FitchLaw

Copyright 2018 FitchLaw. All rights reserved. No part of this publication may be stored in a retrieval system, transmitted, or reproduced in any way, including but not limited to photocopy, photographs, magnetic, or other record, without the prior agreement and written permission of the publisher.

The author and publisher have made their best efforts to prepare this book. The author and publisher make no representation or warranties of any kind with regards to the completeness or accuracy of the contents herein and accepts no liability of any kind, including but not limited to performance, merchantability, fitness for any particular purpose or any losses or damages of any kind caused or alleged to be caused directly or indirectly from this book.
Trademarks:

FitchLaw Inc., has attempted throughout this book to distinguish proprietary trademarks from descriptive terms by following the capitalization style used by the manufacturer.

Published by: FitchLaw Inc.

FitchLaw Inc., welcome corrections and comments on its documents. In addition to comments, please send comments on typographical, formatting, or other errors. Simply make a copy of the relevant page, mark the error, and send it to fitchlawupdates@gmail.com.

Books and testing materials are available at special quantity discounts to use as premiums and sales promotions, or for corporate training programs, as well as other educational programs.

Printed in the United States of America. No part of this work may be reproduced or transmitted in any form or by any means, electronic, manual, photocopying, recording, or by any information storage and retrieval systems, without prior written permission of the publisher.

ISBN-13: 978-1986181266 (paperback)

# Contents

1 **Very Short Overview** — 15

2 **Overview** — 17
   2.1 Classical and Modern Contract Law — 17
   2.2 Consideration — 17
      2.2.1 Donative Promises — 17
      2.2.2 Form — 18
      2.2.3 Reliance and Promissory Estoppel — 18
      2.2.4 The Bargain Principle — 19
      2.2.5 Unconscionability — 19
      2.2.6 Mutuality — 20
      2.2.7 Legal Duty — 21
      2.2.8 Modification — 21
      2.2.9 Waiver — 22
      2.2.10 Past Consideration — 22
      2.2.11 The Limits of Contract — 23
   2.3 Remedies — 23
      2.3.1 Overview — 23
      2.3.2 Expectation Damages — 24
      2.3.3 Specific Performance — 29
      2.3.4 Reliance Damages — 29
      2.3.5 Restitution Damages — 30
   2.4 Assent — 31
      2.4.1 Interpretation — 31
      2.4.2 Offer and Revocation — 32
      2.4.3 Modes of Acceptance — 36
      2.4.4 Implied-in-Law and Implied-in-Fact Contracts — 38
      2.4.5 Preliminary Negotiations, Indefiniteness, and the Duty to Bargain in Good Faith — 39
      2.4.6 Parol Evidence — 40
      2.4.7 Plain Meaning — 43
   2.5 Form Contracts — 43
   2.6 Mistake and Unexpected Circumstances — 45
   2.7 Berring's Basic Rules — 47

3 **Introduction** — 48
   3.1 Rawls, "A Theory of Justice" — 48
   3.2 Scanlon, "Promises and Practices" — 48
   3.3 Gardner, "Observations in the Course of Contracts" — 49

# 4 Consideration — 50

## 4.1 Donative Promises, Form, and Reliance — 50
### 4.1.1 Donative Promises — 50
- 4.1.1.1 Gifts: *Dougherty v. Salt* — 50
- 4.1.1.2 Restatement Second § 1: Definition — 51
- 4.1.1.3 Restatement Second § 17: Requirement of a Bargain — 51
- 4.1.1.4 Restatement Second § 71: Requirement of Exchange; Types of Exchange — 51
- 4.1.1.5 Restatement Second § 79: Adequacy of Consideration; Mutuality of Obligation — 51
- 4.1.1.6 On the Restatement Second — 51
- 4.1.1.7 Consideration — 52
- 4.1.1.8 Gifts — 52
- 4.1.1.9 Donative Promises — 53
- 4.1.1.10 Conditional Donative Promises — 53

### 4.1.2 Form — 54
- 4.1.2.1 Von Mehren, "Civil-Law Analogues to Consideration: An Exercise in Comparative Analysis" — 54
- 4.1.2.2 Channeling Function of Contract-Law Rules — 54
- 4.1.2.3 No Enforcement without Consideration: *Schnell v. Nell* — 54
- 4.1.2.4 Form — 55

### 4.1.3 Reliance and Promissory Estoppel — 55
- 4.1.3.1 No Reliance in Traditional Common Law: *Kirksey v. Kirksey* — 55
- 4.1.3.2 Restatement Second § 90: Promise Reasonably Inducing Action or Forbearance — 56
- 4.1.3.3 Estoppel in Pais and Promissory Estoppel — 56
- 4.1.3.4 Promissory Estoppel Problem — 57
- 4.1.3.5 Promissory Estoppel: *Feinberg v. Pfeiffer Co.* — 57
- 4.1.3.6 Distinguishing *Feinberg*: *Hayes v. Plantations Steel Co.* — 58
- 4.1.3.7 Remedies and Consideration — 59
- 4.1.3.8 *Goldstick v. ICM Realty* — 60
- 4.1.3.9 Reliance Damages vs. Expectation Damages: *D & G Stout, Inc. v. Bacardi Imports, Inc.* — 60
- 4.1.3.10 Promissory Estoppel and Expectation Damages: *Walters v. Marathon Oil Co.* — 61

## 4.2 The Bargain Principle — 61
### 4.2.1 The Bargain Principle — 61
- 4.2.1.1 Benefit and Detriment: *Hamer v. Sidway* — 62
- 4.2.1.2 Statute of Frauds — 62
- 4.2.1.3 Defining Detriment: *Davies v. Martel Laboratory Services, Inc.* — 62

|  |  |  |  |
|---|---|---|---|
|  | 4.2.1.4 | Bad (or Great) Deals: *Hancock Bank & Trust Co. v. Shell Oil Co.* | 63 |
|  | 4.2.1.5 | Restatement Second § 71: Requirements of Exchange; Types of Exchange | 63 |
|  | 4.2.1.6 | Restatement Second § 72: Exchange of Promise for Performance | 63 |
|  | 4.2.1.7 | Restatement Second § 79: Adequacy of Consideration; Mutuality of Obligation | 63 |
|  | 4.2.1.8 | Selling Money: *Batsakis v. Demotsis* | 64 |
|  | 4.2.1.9 | Sweet-Escott, Greece—A Political and Economic Survey, 1939–1953 | 64 |
|  | 4.2.1.10 | Consideration and Remedies | 64 |
|  | 4.2.1.11 | Restatement Second § 175: When Duress by Threat Makes a Contract Voidable | 65 |
|  | 4.2.1.12 | Restatement Second § 176: When a Threat is Improper | 65 |
|  | 4.2.1.13 | UNIDROIT Principles of International Commercial Contracts Art. 3.9: Threat | 65 |
|  | 4.2.1.14 | Principles of European Contract Law § 4.108: Threats | 65 |
|  | 4.2.1.15 | Duress: *Chouinard v. Chouinard* | 66 |
|  | 4.2.1.16 | Rescue and Salvage: *Post v. Jones* | 66 |
|  | 4.2.1.17 | Eisenberg, "The Bargain Principle and Its Limits" | 67 |
|  | 4.2.1.18 | New York Gen. Bus. Law § 396-r: Price Gouging | 67 |
|  | 4.2.1.19 | Price Gouging: *People v. Two Wheel Corp.* | 67 |
| 4.2.2 | Unconscionability | | 67 |
|  | 4.2.2.1 | Lack of Meaningful Choice: *Williams v. Walker-Thomas Furniture Co.* | 67 |
|  | 4.2.2.2 | UCC § 2-302: Unconscionable Contract or Clause | 68 |
|  | 4.2.2.3 | Uniform Consumer Credit Code § 5.108: Unconscionability | 68 |
|  | 4.2.2.4 | Federal Trade Commission Regulations—Door-to-Door Sales | 68 |
|  | 4.2.2.5 | The Uniform Commercial Code | 68 |
|  | 4.2.2.6 | Applying the UCC: *Pittsley v. Houser* | 69 |
|  | 4.2.2.7 | Comments to the UCC | 69 |
|  | 4.2.2.8 | UNIDROIT Principles of International Commercial Contracts Art. 3.10: Gross Disparity | 69 |
|  | 4.2.2.9 | Principles of European Contract Law §§ 4.109, 4.110 | 69 |
|  | 4.2.2.10 | Commission of the European Communities, Council Directive 93/13/EEC | 69 |
|  | 4.2.2.11 | Substantive and Procedural Unconscionability: *Maxwell v. Fidelity Fin. Servs., Inc.* | 69 |
|  | 4.2.2.12 | Classical and Modern Contract Law | 70 |
| 4.2.3 | Mutuality | | 71 |

- 4.2.3.1 Corbin, "The Effect of Options on Consideration" ... 71
- 4.2.3.2 Williston on Contracts § 103B ... 71
- 4.2.3.3 Restatement Second § 77: Illusory and Alternative Promises ... 71
- 4.2.3.4 Illusory Promises ... 71
- 4.2.3.5 Unequal Terms: *Lindner v. Mid-Continent Petroleum Corp.* ... 72
- 4.2.3.6 Reluctant Seller, Eager Buyer: *Gurfein v. Werbelovsky* ... 72
- 4.2.3.7 Satisfaction Clauses: *Mattei v. Hopper* ... 72
- 4.2.3.8 No Equivalence Required for Consideration: *Harris v. Time, Inc.* ... 73
- 4.2.3.9 "Primitive Stage of Formalism": *Wood v. Lucy, Lady Duff-Gordon* ... 73
- 4.2.3.10 UCC § 2-306: Output, Requirements, and Exclusive Dealings ... 73
- 4.2.3.11 Requirements and Output Contracts ... 73
- 4.2.4 Legal Duty, Modification, and Waiver ... 74
  - 4.2.4.1 No Enforcement for Legal Duty: *Slattery v. Wells Fargo Armored Serv. Corp.* ... 74
  - 4.2.4.2 *Shadwell v. Shadwell* ... 74
  - 4.2.4.3 Restatement Second § 73: Performance of Legal Duty ... 74
  - 4.2.4.4 N.Y. Penal Law §§ 200.30, 200.35 ... 74
  - 4.2.4.5 Thin Line Between Legal Duty and No Duty: *Denney v. Reppert* ... 75
  - 4.2.4.6 Extortion is not Consideration: *Lingenfelder v. Wainwright Brewery Co.* ... 75
  - 4.2.4.7 Extortion and Legal Duty: *Austin Instrument, Inc. v. Loral Corp.* ... 75
  - 4.2.4.8 More on the Legal Duty Rule ... 76
  - 4.2.4.9 Substitute Contracts: *Schwartzreich v. Bauman-Basch, Inc.* ... 76
  - 4.2.4.10 Restatement First § 406, Illustration 1 ... 76
  - 4.2.4.11 UCC §§ 3-103(a)(4), 3-104, 3-311 ... 76
  - 4.2.4.12 Restatement Second § 279: Substituted Contract ... 76
  - 4.2.4.13 Restatement Second § 281: Accord and Satisfaction ... 76
  - 4.2.4.14 The Legal Effect of the "Executory Accord" ... 76
  - 4.2.4.15 Restatement Second § 89: Modification of Executory Contract ... 77
  - 4.2.4.16 No Consideration for Modification: *Angel v. Murray* ... 78
  - 4.2.4.17 UCC § 2-209: Modification, Rescission, and Waiver ... 78
  - 4.2.4.18 CISG Art. 29 ... 78
  - 4.2.4.19 Waiver: *Clark v. West* ... 78

# CONTENTS

|  |  |  |  |
|---|---|---|---|
|  |  | 4.2.4.20 Restatement Second § 84: Promise to Perform a Duty in Spite of Non-Occurrence of a Condition | 79 |
|  |  | 4.2.4.21 *Nassau Trust Co. v. Montrose Concrete Prods. Corp.* | 79 |
|  |  | 4.2.4.22 Waiver under the UCC: *BMC Indus., Inc. v. Barth Indus., Inc.* | 79 |
| 4.3 | Past Consideration | | 79 |
|  | 4.3.1 | Restatement Second § 82: Promise to Pay Indebtedness; Effect on the Statute of Limitations | 79 |
|  | 4.3.2 | Restatement Second § 83: Promise to Pay Indebtedness Discharged in Bankruptcy | 80 |
|  | 4.3.3 | Three Situations in Which a Promise to Discharge an Unenforceable Obligation is Binding | 80 |
|  | 4.3.4 | No Past Consideration: *Mills v. Wyman* | 80 |
|  | 4.3.5 | Protection as Consideration: *Webb v. McGowin* | 81 |
|  | 4.3.6 | Saving from Decapitation: *Harrington v. Taylor* | 81 |
|  | 4.3.7 | Restatement Second § 86: Promise for Benefit Received | 81 |
|  | 4.3.8 | ALI 42d Annual Proceedings | 81 |
|  | 4.3.9 | Note on Past Consideration | 82 |
| 4.4 | The Limits of Contract | | 82 |
|  | 4.4.1 | *Balfour v. Balfour* | 82 |
|  | 4.4.2 | In Vitro Fertilization: *In Re the Marriage of Witten* | 82 |
|  | 4.4.3 | Who is a Parent? | 83 |
|  | 4.4.4 | Surrogacy Agreements: *R.R. v. M.H.* | 83 |
|  | 4.4.5 | Surrogate-Parenting Legislation | 84 |
|  | 4.4.6 | 42 U.S. Code § 274e: Prohibition of Organ Purchases | 84 |
|  | 4.4.7 | Radin, "Market-Inalienability" | 84 |

## 5 Remedies — 85

| 5.1 | Introduction to Contract Damages | | 85 |
|---|---|---|---|
|  | 5.1.1 | Restatement Second § 344: Purposes of Remedies | 85 |
|  | 5.1.2 | Expectation Damages: *Hawkins v. McGee* | 85 |
|  | 5.1.3 | Cooter & Eisenberg, "Damages for Breach of Contract" | 86 |
|  | 5.1.4 | Actual Losses and Punitive Damages: *U.S. Naval Inst. v. Charter Commc'ns, Inc.* | 88 |
|  | 5.1.5 | Profiting from Breach: *Coppola Enters., Inc. v. Alfone* | 89 |
|  | 5.1.6 | Diminution in Value: *Laurin v. DeCarolis Constr. Co.* | 89 |
|  | 5.1.7 | The Theory of Efficient Breach | 90 |
|  | 5.1.8 | Rejecting Efficient Breach: *Greer Props., Inc. v. LaSalle Nat'l Bank* | 90 |
| 5.2 | The Expectation Measure | | 91 |
|  | 5.2.1 | Damages for Breach of a Contract to Perform Services | 91 |
|  |  | 5.2.1.1 Cost of Completion: *Louise Caroline Nursing Home, Inc. v. Dix Construction Co.* | 91 |
|  |  | 5.2.1.2 Formulas | 91 |

|         |           |                                                                                                         |     |
|---------|-----------|---------------------------------------------------------------------------------------------------------|----|
|         | 5.2.1.3   | Diminution in Value: *Peevyhouse v. Garland Coal & Mining Co.*                                          | 92  |
|         | 5.2.1.4   | Affirming the *Peevyhouse* Rule: *Schneberger v. Apache Corp.*                                          | 92  |
|         | 5.2.1.5   | Grossly Disproportionate: *H.P. Droher & Sons v. Toushin*                                               | 93  |
|         | 5.2.1.6   | Waste: *Eastern Steamship Lines, Inc. v. United States*                                                 | 93  |
|         | 5.2.1.7   | Aesthetics and Good Faith: *City School Dist. of the City of Elmira v. McLane Const. Co.*               | 93  |
|         | 5.2.1.8   | Residential vs. Commercial Construction: *Fox v. Webb*                                                  | 94  |
|         | 5.2.1.9   | Measuring Diminished Value: *Grossman Holdings Ltd. v. Hourihan*                                        | 94  |
|         | 5.2.1.10  | Factfinder's Discretion: *Advanced, Inc. v. Wilks*                                                      | 94  |
|         | 5.2.1.11  | "Pleasure and Amenity" Damages: *Ruxley Electronics & Construction Ltd. v. Forsyth*                     | 94  |
|         | 5.2.1.12  | Calculating Damages: *Aiello Const., Inc. v. Nationwide Tractor Trailer Training and Placement Corp.*   | 95  |
|         | 5.2.1.13  | *Formulas for Measuring Damages for Breach by a Person Who has Contracted to Have Services Performed*   | 95  |
|         | 5.2.1.14  | Restatement Second § 347: Measure of Damages in General                                                 | 95  |
|         | 5.2.1.15  | Multiple Contracts: *Wired Music, Inc. v. Clark*                                                        | 95  |
|         | 5.2.1.16  | Overhead: *Vitex Mfg. Corp. v. Caribtex Corp.*                                                          | 95  |
| 5.2.2   | Damages for Breach of a Contract for the Sale of Goods: *Seller's* Breach                                           | 96  |
|         | 5.2.2.1   | Cost of Repair Exceeds Purchase Price: *Continental Sand & Gravel, Inc. v. K & K Sand & Gravel, Inc.*   | 96  |
|         | 5.2.2.2   | Direct Damages for Breach of Warranty: *Manouchehri v. Heim*                                            | 96  |
|         | 5.2.2.3   | Cover: *Egerer v. CSR West, LLC*                                                                        | 97  |
|         | 5.2.2.4   | *Panhandle Agri-Service, Inc. v. Becker*                                                                | 97  |
|         | 5.2.2.5   | J. White & R. Summers, "Uniform Commercial Code"                                                        | 98  |
|         | 5.2.2.6   | The Availability of Market-Price Damages to a Buyer Who Has Covered                                     | 98  |
|         | 5.2.2.7   | Incidental Damages: *Delchi Carrier SpA v. Rotorex Corp.*                                               | 98  |
| 5.2.3   | Damages for Breach of a Contract for the Sale of Goods: *Buyer's* Breach                                            | 99  |
|         | 5.2.3.1   | *KGM Harvesting Co. v. Fresh Network*                                                                   | 99  |

|         | 5.2.3.2 | Recovery for Lost Profits under the UCC: *Neri v. Retail Marine Corp.* | 100 |
|---|---|---|---|
|         | 5.2.3.3 | *Teradyne, Inc. v. Teledyne Industries, Inc.* | 101 |
|         | 5.2.3.4 | Childres and Burgess, "Seller's Remedies: The Primacy of UCC 2-708(2)" | 101 |
|         | 5.2.3.5 | *R.E. Davis Chemical Corp. v. Diasonics, Inc.* | 101 |
|         | 5.2.3.6 | Lost Profits for Second-Hand Cars: *Lazenby Garages Ltd. v. Wright* | 102 |
| 5.2.4   | Mitigation; Contracts for Employment | | 102 |
|         | 5.2.4.1 | Duty to Mitigate: *Rockingham County v. Luten Bridge Co.* | 102 |
|         | 5.2.4.2 | Duty to Mitigate for Modified Products: *Madsen v. Murray & Sons, Co.* | 103 |
|         | 5.2.4.3 | Reasonable Mitigation: *In Re Kellet Aircraft Corp.* | 103 |
|         | 5.2.4.4 | "Slight Expense and Reasonable Effort" in Mitigating: *Bank One, Texas N.A. v. Taylor* | 103 |
|         | 5.2.4.5 | Defendant's Mitigation: *S.J. Groves & Sons Co. v. Warner Co.* | 103 |
|         | 5.2.4.6 | Employees' Duty to Mitigate: *Shirley MacLaine Parker v. Twentieth Century-Fox Film Corp.* | 104 |
|         | 5.2.4.7 | *Punkar v. King Plastic Corp.* | 104 |
|         | 5.2.4.8 | Reasonable Expenses in Mitigation: *Mr. Eddie, Inc. v. Ginsberg* | 105 |
|         | 5.2.4.9 | Mitigation through Inferior Employment: *Southern Keswick, Inc. v. Whetherholt* | 105 |
|         | 5.2.4.10 | Damages for Loss of Opportunity to Practice One's Profession | 105 |
| 5.2.5   | Foreseeability | | 105 |
|         | 5.2.5.1 | Reasonably Foreseeable Damages and Special Circumstances: *Hadley v. Baxendale* | 105 |
|         | 5.2.5.2 | Commercial Breach: *Victoria Laundry (Windsor) Ltd. v. Newman Indus. Ltd.* | 106 |
|         | 5.2.5.3 | Market Fluctuations: *Koufos v. C. Czarnikow, Ltd. (The Heron II)* | 106 |
|         | 5.2.5.4 | Commercial Machinery: *Hector Martinez & Co. v. Southern Pacific Transp. Co.* | 106 |
|         | 5.2.5.5 | The Scope of Hadley v. Baxendale | 107 |
| 5.2.6   | Certainty | | 107 |
|         | 5.2.6.1 | *Kenford Co. v. Erie County* | 107 |
|         | 5.2.6.2 | *Ashland Management Inc. v. Janien* | 108 |
|         | 5.2.6.3 | The New-Business Rule | 108 |
|         | 5.2.6.4 | Consistency of Past Performance: *Rombola v. Cosindas* | 108 |
|         | 5.2.6.5 | Statistics of Similar Businesses: *Contemporary Mission, Inc. v. Famous Music Corp.* | 108 |

|  |  | 5.2.6.6 | Uncertainty . . . . . . . . . . . . . . . . . . . . | 108 |
|---|---|---|---|---|

- 5.2.7 Liquidated Damages . . . . . . . . . . . . . . . . . . . . . . . 109
  - 5.2.7.1 Reasonable Approximation: *Wasserman's Inc. v. Middletown* . . . . . . . . . . . . . . . . . . . 109
  - 5.2.7.2 Provisions that Limit Damages . . . . . . . . . 109
- 5.3 Specific Performance . . . . . . . . . . . . . . . . . . . . . . . . . . . . 110
  - 5.3.0.3 Law & Equity . . . . . . . . . . . . . . . . . . . 110
  - 5.3.0.4 *London Bucket Co. v. Stewart* . . . . . . . . . 110
  - 5.3.0.5 Injunction vs. Damages: *Walgreen Co. v. Sara Creek Property Co.* . . . . . . . . . . . . . . . . 110
  - 5.3.0.6 *Stokes v. Moore* . . . . . . . . . . . . . . . . . 111
  - 5.3.0.7 Uniqueness and Uncertainty: *Van Wagner Advertising Corp. v. S & M Enterprises* . . . . . . 111
- 5.4 The Reliance and Restitution Measures . . . . . . . . . . . . . . . 112
  - 5.4.1 Reliance Damages in a Bargain Context . . . . . . . . . . 112
    - 5.4.1.1 *Security Stove & Mfg. Co. v. American Rys. Express Co.* . . . . . . . . . . . . . . . . . . . . 112
    - 5.4.1.2 *Anglia Television Co. v. Reed* . . . . . . . . . 112
    - 5.4.1.3 *Beefy Trail, Inc. v. Beefy King Int'l, Inc.* . . . 113
    - 5.4.1.4 *L. Albert & Son v. Armstrong Rubber Co.* . . . 113
    - 5.4.1.5 *C.C.C. Films (London) v. Impact Quadrant Films Ltd.* . . . . . . . . . . . . . . . . . . . . . . . . 113
    - 5.4.1.6 *Westside Galvanizing Servs., Inc. v. Georgia-Pacific Corp.* . . . . . . . . . . . . . . . . . . . 113
  - 5.4.2 The Restitution Measure . . . . . . . . . . . . . . . . . . . 114
    - 5.4.2.1 *Osteen v. Johnson* . . . . . . . . . . . . . . . . 114
    - 5.4.2.2 Quantum Meruit: *United States v. Algernon Blair, Inc.* . . . . . . . . . . . . . . . . . . . . . 114
    - 5.4.2.3 *Oliver v. Campbell* . . . . . . . . . . . . . . . 115
    - 5.4.2.4 G. Palmer, "The Law of Restitution" . . . . . . 115
    - 5.4.2.5 Restitution and Reliance Damages . . . . . . . . 115
    - 5.4.2.6 Expectation as a Cap on Reliance Damages . . . 115
    - 5.4.2.7 Recovery for the Breaching Party: *Kutzin v. Pirnie* . . . . . . . . . . . . . . . . . . . . . . . 116
    - 5.4.2.8 *United States Ex Rel. Palmer Const., Inc. v. Cal State Electric, Inc.* . . . . . . . . . . . . . 117
    - 5.4.2.9 *R.J. Berke & Co. v. Griffin, Inc.* . . . . . . . . 117
    - 5.4.2.10 *Vines v. Orchard Hills, Inc.* . . . . . . . . . . 117

# 6 Assent  118
- 6.1 Introduction to Interpretation . . . . . . . . . . . . . . . . . . . . 118
  - 6.1.1 Subjectivity and Objectivity . . . . . . . . . . . . . . . . . 118
    - 6.1.1.1 Restatement First § 227 . . . . . . . . . . . . . 118
    - 6.1.1.2 Objective Intent: *Lucy v. Zehmer* . . . . . . . 118
    - 6.1.1.3 *Keller v. Holderman* . . . . . . . . . . . . . . 118
    - 6.1.1.4 *Raffles v. Wichelhaus* . . . . . . . . . . . . . . 119

|        |       | 6.1.1.5  | Simpson, "Contracts for Cotton to Arrive: The Case of the Two Ships *Peerless* . . . . . . . . . . | 119 |
|---|---|---|---|---|
|        |       | 6.1.1.6  | "Chicken": *Frigaliment Importing Co. v. B.N.S. Intern. Sales Co.* . . . . . . . . . . . . . . . . | 119 |
|        |       | 6.1.1.7  | *Oswald v. Allen* . . . . . . . . . . . . . . . . | 119 |
|        |       | 6.1.1.8  | *Falck v. Williams* . . . . . . . . . . . . . . | 119 |
|        |       | 6.1.1.9  | *Colfax Envelope Corp. v. Local No. 458-3M* | 120 |
|        |       | 6.1.1.10 | Intent: *Embry v. Hargadine, McKittrick Dry Goods Co.* . . . . . . . . . . . . . . . . . . | 120 |
|        |       | 6.1.1.11 | CISG and Intent: *MCC-Marble Ceramic Center, Inc. v. Ceramica Nuova D'Agostino* . . . . | 120 |
|        |       | 6.1.1.12 | *Mayol v. Weiner Companies, Ltd.* . . . . . . . | 121 |
|        |       | 6.1.1.13 | Objective and Subjective Elements in Interpretation . . . . . . . . . . . . . . . . . . . . . | 121 |
|        |       | 6.1.1.14 | *Berke Moore Co. v. Phoenix Bridge Co.* . . . . | 121 |
|        | 6.1.2 | Problems of Interpreting Purposive Language . . . . . . . | 122 |
|        |       | 6.1.2.1  | Fish, "Normal Circumstances, Literal Language, Direct Speech Acts, the Ordinary, the Everyday, the Obvious, What Goes Without Saying, and Other Special Cases" . . . . . . . . . . . . . . | 122 |
|        |       | 6.1.2.2  | *Haines v. New York* . . . . . . . . . . . . . . | 122 |
|        |       | 6.1.2.3  | *Spaulding v. Morse* . . . . . . . . . . . . . . | 122 |
|        |       | 6.1.2.4  | *Lawson v. Martin Timber Co.* . . . . . . . . . | 122 |
|        |       | 6.1.2.5  | Lieber, "Legal and Political Hermeneutics" . . . | 122 |
|        | 6.1.3 | Usage, Course of Dealing, and Course of Performance . . | 123 |
|        |       | 6.1.3.1  | Trade Usage: *Foxco Industries, Ltd. v. Fabric World, Inc.* . . . . . . . . . . . . . . . . . . | 123 |
|        |       | 6.1.3.2  | Trade Quantities: *Hurst v. W.J. Lake & Co.* . . | 123 |
|        |       | 6.1.3.3  | *Flower City Painting Contractors, Inc. v. Gumina* . . . . . . . . . . . . . . . . . . . . . | 123 |
|        |       | 6.1.3.4  | J. White & R. Summers, UCC § 1-2 . . . . . . . | 123 |
| 6.2    | Offer and Revocation . . . . . . . . . . . . . . . . . . . . . . . . | | | 123 |
|        | 6.2.1 | What Constitutes an Offer . . . . . . . . . . . . . . . . | 123 |
|        |       | 6.2.1.1  | *Lonergan v. Scolnick* . . . . . . . . . . . . . | 123 |
|        |       | 6.2.1.2  | *Regent Lighting Corp. v. CMT Corp.* . . . . . | 123 |
|        |       | 6.2.1.3  | Unilateral Offer: *Lefkowitz v. Great Minneapolis Surplus Store* . . . . . . . . . . . . . . . . | 123 |
|        |       | 6.2.1.4  | Limits on Unilateral Offer: *Ford Motor Credit Co. v. Russell* . . . . . . . . . . . . . . . . | 124 |
|        |       | 6.2.1.5  | *Donovan v. RRL Corp.* . . . . . . . . . . . . | 124 |
|        |       | 6.2.1.6  | *Fisher v. Bell* . . . . . . . . . . . . . . . . | 124 |
|        |       | 6.2.1.7  | Auctions for Sale of Land: *Hoffman v. Horton* . | 124 |
|        |       | 6.2.1.8  | Auctions . . . . . . . . . . . . . . . . . . . . | 124 |
|        |       | 6.2.1.9  | Note on Offer and Acceptance . . . . . . . . . | 124 |
|        | 6.2.2 | Lapse, Rejection, and Counter-Offer . . . . . . . . . . . | 125 |
|        |       | 6.2.2.1  | *Akers v. J.B. Sedberry, Inc.* . . . . . . . . . . | 125 |

|  |  | 6.2.2.2 | *Effect of the Rejection of an Offer* . . . . . . . . 125 |
|---|---|---|---|
|  |  | 6.2.2.3 | Qualified vs. Absolute Acceptance: *Ardente v. Horan* . . . . . . . . . . . . . . . . . . . . . . . . 125 |
|  |  | 6.2.2.4 | Benficial Condition: *Rhode Island Dep't of Transp. v. Providence & Worcester R.R.* . . . . . . . . . 126 |
|  |  | 6.2.2.5 | Grumbling Acceptance: *Price v. Oklahoma College of Osteopathic Medicine and Surgery* . . . . 126 |
|  |  | 6.2.2.6 | Mirror-Image Rule . . . . . . . . . . . . . . . . 126 |
|  |  | 6.2.2.7 | Renewal by Implication: *Livingstone v. Evans* . 126 |
|  |  | 6.2.2.8 | *Culton v. Gilchrist* . . . . . . . . . . . . . . . 127 |
|  |  | 6.2.2.9 | Effect of the Offeror's Death or Incapacity Before Acceptance . . . . . . . . . . . . . . . . . 127 |
|  | 6.2.3 | Revocation . . . . . . . . . . . . . . . . . . . . . . . . . 127 |  |
|  |  | 6.2.3.1 | What Constitutes Receipt of Written Acceptance? 127 |
|  |  | 6.2.3.2 | Preparing for Performance: *Ragosta v. Wilder* . 127 |
|  |  | 6.2.3.3 | Offers for Unilateral Contracts . . . . . . . . . . 128 |
|  |  | 6.2.3.4 | Reliance and Revocability: *Drennan v. Star Paving Co.* . . . . . . . . . . . . . . . . . . . . 128 |
|  |  | 6.2.3.5 | Critiques of *Drennan*: *Pavel Enterprises, Inc. v. A.S. Johnson Co. 452* . . . . . . . . . . . . . 129 |
|  |  | 6.2.3.6 | Dodge, "Teaching the CISG in Contracts" . . . 130 |
|  |  | 6.2.3.7 | Limiting *Drennan*: *Preload Technology, Inc. v. A.B. & J. Construction Co., Inc.* . . . . . . . . 130 |
|  |  | 6.2.3.8 | Restatement Second § 87(2): Option Contract . 130 |
| 6.3 | Modes of Acceptance . . . . . . . . . . . . . . . . . . . . . . . . 131 |  |  |
|  | 6.3.1 | Acceptance by Act . . . . . . . . . . . . . . . . . . . . . 131 |  |
|  |  | 6.3.1.1 | Promise to Bequeath: *Klockner v. Green* . . . . 131 |
|  |  | 6.3.1.2 | Diamond Jim: *Simmons v. United States* . . . . 131 |
|  |  | 6.3.1.3 | *Stephens v. Memphis* . . . . . . . . . . . . . . 132 |
|  |  | 6.3.1.4 | Performance of a Condition as Acceptance: *Carlill v. Carbolic Smoke Ball, Inc.* . . . . . . . . . . 132 |
|  | 6.3.2 | Subjective Acceptance . . . . . . . . . . . . . . . . . . . 133 |  |
|  |  | 6.3.2.1 | *International Filter Co. v. Conroe Gin, Ince, & Light Co.* . . . . . . . . . . . . . . . . . . . . . 133 |
|  | 6.3.3 | Acceptance by Conduct . . . . . . . . . . . . . . . . . . 133 |  |
|  |  | 6.3.3.1 | Regular Conduct as Tacit Assent: *Polaroid Corp. v. Rollins Environmental Services (NJ), Inc.* . . 133 |
|  | 6.3.4 | The Effect of Using a Subcontractor's Bid . . . . . . . . 134 |  |
|  |  | 6.3.4.1 | *Holman Erection Co. v. Orville E. Madsen & Sons, Inc.* . . . . . . . . . . . . . . . . . . . . . 134 |
|  |  | 6.3.4.2 | *Southern California Acoustics, Inc. v. C.V. Holder, Inc.* . . . . . . . . . . . . . . . . . . . . 135 |
|  | 6.3.5 | Silence As Acceptance . . . . . . . . . . . . . . . . . . . 135 |  |
|  |  | 6.3.5.1 | *Vogt v. Madden* . . . . . . . . . . . . . . . . . 135 |
|  |  | 6.3.5.2 | *Laurel Race Courses v. Regal Const. Co.* . . . . 135 |
|  |  | 6.3.5.3 | *Cole-McIntyre-Norfleet Co. v. Holloway* . . . . 136 |

|  |  |  |  |
|---|---|---|---|
|  |  | 6.3.5.4 | Duty to Promptly Reply: *Kukusa v. Home Mut. Hail-Tornado Ins. Co.* . . . . . . . . . . . . . . . . 136 |
|  |  | 6.3.5.5 | Standing Offer: *Hobbs v. Massasoit Whip Co.* . . 136 |
|  |  | 6.3.5.6 | *Louisville Tin & Stove Co. v. Lay* . . . . . . . . 136 |
|  |  | 6.3.5.7 | *Austin v. Burge* . . . . . . . . . . . . . . . . . . 136 |
|  |  | 6.3.5.8 | Negative-Option Plans . . . . . . . . . . . . . 137 |
|  |  | 6.3.5.9 | The Significance of Unjust Enrichment and Loss through Reliance in Cases Where Silence Is Treated as Acceptance . . . . . . . . . . . . . . . . . . 137 |
|  | 6.3.6 | Acceptance by Electronic Agent | . . . . . . . . . . . . . 137 |

6.4 Implied-in-Law and Implied-in-Fact Contracts; Unilateral Contracts Revisited . . . . . . . . . . . . . . . . . . . . . . . . . . . . . . . . 137
    6.4.1 Contract Implied in Law: *Nursing Care Services, Inc. v. Dobos* . . . . . . . . . . . . . . . . . . . . . . . . . . . . . 137
    6.4.2 *Sceva v. True* . . . . . . . . . . . . . . . . . . . . . . . . 138
    6.4.3 Implied-in-Fact and Implied-in-Law Contracts . . . . . . . 138
    6.4.4 Morrison, "I Imply What You Infer Unless You Are a Court" 138
    6.4.5 *Day v. Caton* . . . . . . . . . . . . . . . . . . . . . . . . 138
    6.4.6 Distinguishing Implied-in-Law and Implied-in-Fact: *Bastian v. Gafford* . . . . . . . . . . . . . . . . . . . . . . . . 139
    6.4.7 Remedies for Implied Contracts: *Hill v. Waxberg* . . . . . 139
    6.4.8 Unjust Enrichment vs. Quantum Meruit: *Ramsey v. Ellis* 139
    6.4.9 Enforceability of Employee Handbooks: *Pine River State Bank v. Mettille* . . . . . . . . . . . . . . . . . . . . . . . 139
    6.4.10 Modification of Employee Handbooks . . . . . . . . . . . 139
    6.4.11 The Effect of Disclaimers in Employee Handbooks . . . . 139

6.5 Preliminary Negotiations, Indefiniteness, and the Duty to Bargain in Good Faith . . . . . . . . . . . . . . . . . . . . . . . . . . . . 139
    6.5.1 Uncertain and Indefinite: *Academy Chicago Publishers v. Cheever* . . . . . . . . . . . . . . . . . . . . . . . . . . . . 140
    6.5.2 *Ridgway v. Wharton* . . . . . . . . . . . . . . . . . . . . 140
    6.5.3 *Berg Agency v. Sleepworld-Willingboro, Inc.* . . . . . . . 141
    6.5.4 *Rego v. Decker* . . . . . . . . . . . . . . . . . . . . . . . 141
    6.5.5 *AROK Construction Co. v. Indian Construction Services* 141
    6.5.6 *Saliba-Kringlen Corp. v. Allen Engineering Co.* . . . . . . 141
    6.5.7 Gap-Fillers . . . . . . . . . . . . . . . . . . . . . . . . . . 141
    6.5.8 Hawkland, "Sales Contracts Terms under the UCC" . . . 142
    6.5.9 Agreement to Agree: *Joseph Martin, Jr., Delicatessen, Inc. v. Schumacher* . . . . . . . . . . . . . . . . . . . . . 142
    6.5.10 *Moolenaar v. Co-Build Companies, Inc.* . . . . . . . . . . 142
    6.5.11 Good Faith Negotiations: *Channel Home Centers v. Grossman* . . . . . . . . . . . . . . . . . . . . . . . . . . . . . . 143

6.6 The Parol Evidence Rule and the Interpretation of Written Contracts . . . . . . . . . . . . . . . . . . . . . . . . . . . . . . . . . . . 143
    6.6.1 The Parol Evidence Rule . . . . . . . . . . . . . . . . . . 143
        6.6.1.1 Thayer, "A Preliminary Treatise on Evidence" . 143

|  |  | 6.6.1.2 | Calamari & Perillo, "A Plea for a Uniform Parol Evidence Rule and Principles of Interpretation" | 144 |
|---|---|---|---|---|
|  |  | 6.6.1.3 | Restatement First §§ 228, 237, 239, 240 | 144 |
|  |  | 6.6.1.4 | Braucher, "Interpretation and Legal Effect in the Second Restatement of Contracts" | 145 |
|  |  | 6.6.1.5 | *Hatley v. Stafford* | 145 |
|  |  | 6.6.1.6 | *Interform Co. v. Mitchell Constr. Co.* | 145 |
|  |  | 6.6.1.7 | Murray, "The Parol Evidence Process and Standardized Agreements under the Restatement, Second, Contracts" | 145 |
|  |  | 6.6.1.8 | Dodge, "Teaching the CISG in Contracts" | 146 |
|  |  | 6.6.1.9 | *Masterson v. Sine* | 146 |
|  |  | 6.6.1.10 | *Interform v. Mitchell Constr. Co.* | 146 |
|  |  | 6.6.1.11 | *Hunt Foods and Industries, Inc. v. Doliner* | 147 |
|  |  | 6.6.1.12 | *Alaska Northern Development, Inc. v. Alyeska Pipeline Service Co.* | 147 |
|  |  | 6.6.1.13 | Merger Clauses | 147 |
|  |  | 6.6.1.14 | *ARB (American Research Bureau), Inc. v. E-Systems, Inc.* | 147 |
|  |  | 6.6.1.15 | *Siebel v. Layne & Bowler, Inc.* | 148 |
|  |  | 6.6.1.16 | The Fraud Exception to the Parol Evidence Rule | 148 |
|  |  | 6.6.1.17 | The Condition-to-Legal Effectiveness Exception to the Parol Evidence Rule | 148 |
|  |  | 6.6.1.18 | No Oral Modification Clauses | 148 |
|  | 6.6.2 | The Interpretation of Written Contracts | | 149 |
|  |  | 6.6.2.1 | Plain Meaning: *Steuart v. McChesney* | 149 |
|  |  | 6.6.2.2 | *Mellon Bank, N.A. v. Aetna Business Credit, Inc.* | 150 |
|  |  | 6.6.2.3 | *Amoco Production Co. v. Western Slope Gas Co.* | 150 |
|  |  | 6.6.2.4 | *Pacific Gas & Electric Co. v. G.W. Thomas Drayage & Rigging Co.* | 150 |
|  |  | 6.6.2.5 | *Garden State Plaza Corp. v. S.S. Kresge Co.* | 151 |
|  |  | 6.6.2.6 | *Trident Center v. Connecticut General Life Ins. Co.* | 151 |

**7 Form Contracts**     **152**
- 7.1 Contract Formation in a Form-Contract Setting . . . . . . . . . . 152
  - 7.1.1 Battle of the Forms: The Basic Issues . . . . . . . . . . 152
    - 7.1.1.1 What constitutes acceptance under UCC § 2-207? 152
    - 7.1.1.2 *Columbia Hyundai, Inc. v. Carll Hyundai, Inc.* 152
    - 7.1.1.3 "Expressly Conditional": *Gardner Zemke Co. v. Dunham Bush, Inc.* . . . . . . . . . . . . . 153
    - 7.1.1.4 The Meaning of "Materially Alter" under UCC § 2-207(2)(b) . . . . . . . . . . . . . . . . 153
    - 7.1.1.5 The "Expressly Made Conditional" Clause in UCC § 2-207 . . . . . . . . . . . . . . . . 153
- 7.2 "Rolling Contracts" . . . . . . . . . . . . . . . . . . . . . . . . . . 153

|  |  |  |  |  |
|---|---|---|---|---|
|  |  | 7.2.1 | Shrinkwrap Agreements: *ProCD, Inc. v. Zeidenberg* | 153 |
|  |  | 7.2.2 | Applying *ProCD* to Hardware: *Hill v. Gateway 2000* | 154 |
|  |  | 7.2.3 | Clickwrap Agreements: *Specht v. Netscape Communications Corp.* | 155 |
|  | 7.3 | Interpretation and Unconscionability in a Form Contract Setting | | 155 |
|  |  | 7.3.1 | Reformation and Mutual Mistake: *Sardo v. Fidelity & Deposit Co.* | 155 |
|  |  | 7.3.2 | Llewellyn, "The Common Law Tradition: Deciding Appeals" | 156 |
|  |  | 7.3.3 | *Weaver v. American Oil Co.* | 156 |

# 8 Mistake and Unexpected Circumstances — 157

8.1 Mistake . . . 157
    8.1.1 Unilateral Mistakes (Mechanical Errors) . . . 157
        8.1.1.1 The Nolan Ryan Baseball Card Case . . . 157
        8.1.1.2 Unilateral Mistake . . . 157
    8.1.2 Mistakes in Transcription; Reformation . . . 157
        8.1.2.1 *Travelers Ins. Co. v. Bailey* . . . 157
        8.1.2.2 *Chimart Associates v. Paul* . . . 158
    8.1.3 Mutual Mistakes (Shared Mistaken Assumptions) . . . 158
        8.1.3.1 Barren Cow: *Sherwood v. Walker* . . . 158
        8.1.3.2 *Nester v. Michigan Land & Iron Co.* . . . 159
        8.1.3.3 *Griffith v. Brymer* . . . 160
        8.1.3.4 *Wood v. Boynton* . . . 160
        8.1.3.5 *Firestone & Parson, Inc. v. Union League of Philadelphia* . . . 160
        8.1.3.6 *Everett v. Estate of Sumstad* . . . 161
        8.1.3.7 "Basic Assumption": *Lenawee County Board of Health v. Messerly* . . . 161
        8.1.3.8 *Beachcomber Coins, Inc. v. Boskett* . . . 162
8.2 The Effect of Unexpected Circumstances . . . 162
    8.2.1 Implied Condition: *Taylor v. Caldwell* . . . 163
    8.2.2 Tacit Assumptions—Continued . . . 163
    8.2.3 *Ocean Tramp Tankers Corp. v. V/O Sovfracht* . . . 163
    8.2.4 Impracticality: *Mineral Park Land Co. v. Howard* . . . 163
    8.2.5 Bad Gamble: *United States v. Wegematic Corp.* . . . 164
    8.2.6 Commercial Impracticability: *Missouri Public Service Co. v. Peabody Coal Co.* . . . 164
8.3 Problems of Performance . . . 165
    8.3.1 The Obligation to Perform in Good Faith . . . 165
        8.3.1.1 Duty to Avoid Interfering with Performance: *Patterson v. Meyerhofer* . . . 165
        8.3.1.2 Indirect Interference: *Iron Trade Products Co. v. Wilkoff Co.* . . . 165
        8.3.1.3 *Kirke La Shelle Co. v. Paul Armstrong Co.* . . . 165
        8.3.1.4 The UCC Definitions of Good Faith . . . 165

- 8.3.1.5 Duty to Perform in Good Faith under the UCC and Restatement Second . . . . . . . . . . . . . 165
- 8.3.1.6 Farnsworth, "Good Faith in Contract Performance" . . . . . . . . . . . . . . . . . . . . . . . 166

## § 1  Very Short Overview

1. Consideration:

    (a) Donative promises, gifts, conditional donative promises.

    (b) Form.

    (c) Reliance, estoppel in pais, promissory estoppel.

    (d) The bargain principle, adequacy, duress, salvage.

    (e) Unconscionability.

    (f) Mutuality, illusory promises.

    (g) Legal duty, extortion.

    (h) Modification, waiver.

    (i) Past consideration, moral obligations.

2. Remedies:

    (a) Efficient breach.

    (b) Expectation—services, sale of goods (buyer's and seller's breach), mitigation, foreseeability, certainty, liquidated damages.

    (c) Specific performance, uncertainty, uniqueness.

    (d) Reliance.

    (e) Restitution, unjust enrichment, quantum meruit.

3. Assent:

    (a) Offer and revocation:

    　　i. Interpretation—objectivity vs. subjectivity, meeting of the minds, reasonableness, trade usage.

    　　ii. Offer—Negotiation, firm offer, unilateral offer.

    　　iii. Lapse, rejection, qualified acceptance, renewal.

    　　iv. Revocation—unilateral contract rule, consideration/reliance, subcontractors, option contracts.

    (b) Acceptance by act, subjective acceptance, acceptance by conduct, using a subcontractor's bid, silence, electronic agent.

    (c) Implied-in-law, implied-in-fact.

    (d) Preliminary negotiations, indefiniteness, gap-fillers, future agreements, good faith negotiations.

    (e) Parol evidence, lawyer's paradise, Williston vs. Corbin, merger/integration clauses, fraud exception, condition-to-legal-effectiveness exception.

    (f) Plain meaning, Traynor vs. Kozinski.

4. Form contracts:

(a) Battle of the forms, UCC § 2-207 ("expressly conditional"), knockout rule.

(b) Rolling contracts, shrinkwrap agreements, clickwrap agreements.

(c) Reformation, unconscionability.

(d) Llewellyn.

5. Mistake and unexpected circumstances:

    (a) Unilateral mistake/mechanical error, mistake in transcription.

    (b) Mutual mistake, impossibility, *Sherwood*, "basic assumption."

    (c) Unexpected circumstances, implied conditions, tacit assumptions, impracticability.

    (d) Implied covenant of good faith and fair dealing, difficulty of performance.

# § 2 Overview

## 2.1 Classical and Modern Contract Law

1. Contract law reasoning:[1]

    (a) *Substantive legal reasoning*: validity of a doctrine turns on normative considerations (morals, policy, etc.).

    (b) *Formal legal reasoning*: law consists of doctrines that are autonomous from policy, morality, and experience.

    (c) *Axiomatic legal reasoning*: "fundamental doctrines can be established on the ground that they are self-evident."[2]

    (d) *Deductive legal reasoning*: most doctrines follow from syllogisms beginning with more fundamental doctrines.

    (e) Classical contract law coupled axiomatic and deductive reasoning.

    (f) By contrast, modern contract law reasoning justifies doctrines on the basis of morality, policy, and experience.

2. Contract law can be plotted along four axes:

    (a) Objectivity (directly observable state of the world) $\leftrightarrow$ subjectivity (mental state).

    (b) Standardization (depends on abstract variables) $\leftrightarrow$ individualization (depends on situation-specific variables).

    (c) Static (depends on what occurred at the moment the contract was formed) $\leftrightarrow$ dynamic (depends on moving streams of events before and after the contract).

    (d) Binary (e.g., either no damages or full expectation damages) $\leftrightarrow$ multifaceted (e.g., no damages, expectation damages, reliance damages, restitution damages).

3. Many other limits on contracts are surrogates for unconscionability.[3]

## 2.2 Consideration

### 2.2.1 Donative Promises

1. Donative promises are not enforceable. *Dougherty v. Salt*.

2. But, gifts cannot be revoked once given.

---

[1] Casebook p. 83 ff.
[2] Casebook p. 83.
[3] Casebook p. 86.

3. Acceptance alone is not consideration, but at some point, an act of acceptance involves so much effort that it becomes consideration (the "tramp example").

4. Courts generally do not assess the adequacy of consideration.

5. Two conceptions:

    (a) *Broad*: "consideration" refers collectively to the things that make contracts legally enforceable—e.g., bargain or reliance.[4]

    (b) *Narrow*: "consideration" is the same thing as "bargain." The Restatement Second adopts this approach, known as the **bargain theory of consideration**.

6. **Bargain promise**: the condition is the price—e.g., I'll give you $20 if you mow my lawn.

7. **Conditional donative promise**: the condition is the means to make the gift—e.g., I'll buy you a car if you pick one that costs less than $15,000.

### 2.2.2 Form

1. Historically, formal elements (wax seals, etc.) indicated the validity of an agreement. Today, form has little effect.

2. Ritual is not enough. To be valid, consideration must impose a legal obligation. *Schnell v. Nell*.

### 2.2.3 Reliance and Promissory Estoppel

1. Early courts did not recognize reliance as grounds for enforcing an agreement. *Kirksey v. Kirksey* ("Dear Sister Antillico . . . ").

2. **Estoppel in pais** (or equitable estoppel): if A made a statement and B foreseeably relied on that statement, A is estopped from denying that statement's truth. Based on a *statement of fact*.

3. **Promissory estoppel**: a promise is binding if the promisee reasonably relied on it. Based on a *promise*. *Feinberg v. Pfeiffer*. Cf. *Hayes v. Plantations Steel Co.*

    (a) Restatement § 90: "A promise which the promisor should reasonably expect to induce action or forbearance on the part of the promisee or a third person and which does induce such action or forbearance is binding if injustice can be avoided only by enforcement of the promise. The remedy granted for breach **may be limited as justice requires**."

---

[4]Casebook p. 8.

4. Reliance damages can compensate a party for injuries arising from justified reliance. *D & G Stout, Inc. v. Bacardi Imports, Inc.*

5. Courts are hesitant to award expectation damages for lost profits, but they will if the venture was reasonably likely to be profitable. *Walters v. Marathon Oil Co.*

### 2.2.4 The Bargain Principle

1. Consideration arises from a **bargained-for exchange**. Moral obligations are not enough.

2. Courts will not evaluate the adequacy of consideration as long as the consideration created a legal obligation.

3. Consideration can arise from an act or forbearance. *Hamer v. Sidway*, *Davies v. Martel Laboratory Services, Inc.* See Restatement §§ 71, 72, 79.

4. Bad (or great) deals are enforceable if there is consideration. *Hancock Bank & Trust Co. v. Shell Oil Co.*

5. Loan agreements are enforceable even if the amount to be repaid is orders of magnitude larger than the amount loaned. *Batsakis v. Demotsis*.

6. **Duress** will invalidate a contract. But, driving a hard bargain is not wrongful. *Chouinard v. Chouinard*.

7. The rules against duress prevent a rescuer from unfairly profiting from the rescue. However, the rules of **salvage** create an incentive to rescue by rewarding the rescuer and compensating him for his costs, striking a balance between the rescuer's effort and the victim's need. *Post v. Jones*.

    (a) *The Desperate Traveler*: T is stranded in the desert. G passes by and offers a ride for two-thirds of T's wealth or $100,000, whichever is more.

    (b) Classical contract law would enforce the agreement because the rescuer was not responsible for putting the promisor in a position of distress. Salvage rules offer a solution by preventing the rescuer from exploiting the one in distress while also creating an incentive to rescue.

8. Price gouging is wrong.

### 2.2.5 Unconscionability

1. Unconscionability arises when there is a **lack of meaningful choice** and the terms of the agreement are **unreasonable favorable to one party**. Large disparities in bargaining power can also signal unconscionability. *Williams v. Walker-Thomas Furniture Co.*

2. UCC § 2-302: courts can rescind or reform unconscionable contracts. *Accord* Restatement § (invaliding agreements with *gross* disparities in consideration or bargaining power, but holding that imbalances do not always indicate unconscionability).

3. There's no easy way to explain unconscionability. The UCC and the Restatement struggle to define it. As soon as we define it, people will draft around it. But we know it when we see it.

4. **Substantive unconscionability**: one-sidedness.

5. **Procedural unconscionability**: fine-print surprises. *Maxwell v. Fidelity Fin. Servs., Inc.*

### 2.2.6 Mutuality

1. Under classical contract law, there was no contract without mutual benefit and detriment—i.e., both parties must be bound, or neither is.

2. "As a contract defense, the mutuality doctrine has become a faltering rampart to which a litigant retreats at his own peril."[5] *Helle v. Landmark, Inc.*

3. Restatement § 79: if there is consideration, there are no requirements of gain/loss, equivalence in value, or "mutuality of obligation."

4. **Illusory promises**: there is no consideration without commitment. Today, courts will find a lack of mutuality only if one party retains **complete** discretion to abandon the agreement, which rarely occurs. We also require parties to perform in good faith. Today, courts generally look beyond the contract's literal terms to determine whether the parties intended the agreement to be mutually binding. The intent of the parties outweighs **"primitive formalism."** *Wood v. Lucy, Lady Duff-Gordon.*

5. As long as there is sufficient consideration, unequal terms do not invalidate a contract. *Lindner v. Mid-Continent Petroleum Corp.*

6. **Satisfaction clauses** constitute consideration when courts read them as requiring good faith. Otherwise, the satisfaction clause would not involve a commitment, so the promise would be illusory. *Mattei v. Hopper.*

7. Any bargained-for act or forbearance constitutes consideration. But de minimus non curat lex. *Harris v. Time, Inc.*

8. Requirements contracts and output contracts:

    (a) *Requirements contract*: a seller agrees to provide as much of a good as the buyer requires.

---
[5] Casebook p. 100.

## 2 OVERVIEW

  (b) *Output contract*: a buyer agrees to buy all of a seller's output.

  (c) Traditionally, "courts often refused to enforce requirements contracts where the buyer could choose to have no requirements."[6] But both parties shrunk their realm of choice, so there was mutual consideration.

  (d) UCC § 2-306 requires good faith in requirements contracts.

  (e) " . . . a modern court would almost certainly hold that all requirements and output contracts have consideration."

### 2.2.7 Legal Duty

1. Performance of an existing duty is not consideration. *Slattery v. Wells Fargo Armored Serv. Corp.*, but see *Denney v. Reppert*.

2. Withholding performance does not create consideration for a modification. It looks more like extortion. *Lingenfelder v. Wainwright Brewery Co.*

3. The preexisting duty rule helps prevent extortion. *Alaska Packers' Association v. Domenico*. On the other hand, where a modification involves consideration, the preexisting duty rule fails to stop extortion. *Austin Instrument, Inc. v. Loral* (where the court found valid consideration, but nonetheless held for Loral on a theory of duress).

4. The preexisting duty rule can also allow parties to renege on good faith modifications. For example, A hires B to build a house for $100,000. The cost of materials rises during construction. A and B agree to raise the contract price to $150,000. When the job is done, A backs out, claiming (1) that there was no consideration for the modification and (2) that B was performing a preexisting duty.

### 2.2.8 Modification

1. Today, courts generally do not require consideration for good faith modifications. *Schwartzreich v. Bauman-Basch, Inc.*, *Angel v. Murray*.

2. *Accord*: an agreement under which a new obligation replaces an existing obligation.

3. *Executory accord*: an unperformed accord.

4. *Satisfaction*: performance of the accord.

5. **Substituted contract**: the earlier agreement is immediately discharged.

6. Substituted contract vs. accord:

---
[6] Casebook p. 103.

(a) Courts are likely to find that an accord is a substituted contract if the original duty "was disputed, unliquidated, had not matured, and involved a performance other than the payment of money."[7] For instance, for agricultural services, A agreed to pay B in cattle. They disagreed over how many cattle were due. They agreed that A would pay three sheep instead. Courts will likely treat the accord as a substituted contract.

(b) Courts are likely to find that an accord is *not* a substituted contract if the original duty "was undisputed, liquidated, had matured, and involved the payment of money."[8] For instance, A agreed to pay $900 for B's services, and A does not dispute B's claim. They agree that A will give two sheep instead of paying $900. Courts will likely *not* find that the accord is a substituted contract.

7. Restatement § 89: a promise modifying an earlier contract is binding when:

   (a) It's fair;
   (b) Provided by statute; or
   (c) "justice requires enforcement" if a party relies on it.

### 2.2.9 Waiver

1. Parties can waive contractual terms. *Clark v. West.*

2. Courts are split on whether waiver requires reliance. *Nassau Trust Co. v. Montrose Concrete Products Co.*

### 2.2.10 Past Consideration

1. Traditionally, there are **three areas** in which a promise to discharge a prior unenforceable obligation is binding:

   (a) A promise to pay a debt barred by the statute of limitations.
   (b) A promise by an adult to pay a debt incurred when the person was underage.
   (c) A promise to pay a debt that has been discharged in bankruptcy.

2. Moral obligations do not make promises enforceable. Past consideration is required. *Mills v. Wyman, Harrington v. Taylor.* But, equity can compel courts to depart from the rule. *Webb v. McGowin.*

   (a) ALI: past consideration is *sometimes* binding. Some cases are "gratuitous transactions" (with no consideration) and "quasi-contracts" (with consideration, if justice requires).[9]

---
[7] Casebook pp. 136–37.
[8] Casebook p. 137.
[9] Casebook p. 160–61.

## 2 OVERVIEW

3. If A confers a benefit on B without B's prior request, the subsequent relationship could fall into three categories:

    (a) B is **legally obligated** to compensate A under the law of *unjust enrichment*—for instance, if A paid B money by mistake. The Restatement (Second) adopts this approach, though courts traditionally did not recognize it.

    (b) B is **morally but not legally obligated** to compensate A—for instance, if B has suffered a loss on rescuing A. *Mills v. Wyman*.

    (c) B is **neither morally nor legally obligated** to compensate A—e.g., ordinary gifts.

### 2.2.11 The Limits of Contract

1. Agreements do not always constitute a binding agreement—e.g., two people agreeing to go to a party.

2. Should courts enforce in vitro fertilization agreements? Until what point can parties change their minds? *In Re the Marriage of Witten*. What about surrogacy agreements? *R.R. v. M.H.*

3. 42 U.S.C. § 247(e): organs cannot be bought.

4. Posner: any bureaucratic solution will be flawed, so let's allow the sale of organs on the open market.

5. Radin: "In precluding sales but not gifts, market-inalienability places some things outside the marketplace but not outside the realm of social intercourse."[10] Some things shouldn't be commodified—children, organs, sexual services, and so on.

## 2.3 Remedies

### 2.3.1 Overview

1. **Expectation**: puts promisee in the position he would have been in if the contract had been *performed*. You get what you bargained for.

2. **Reliance**: puts promisee in the position he would have been in if the contract had *not been made*.

3. **Restitution**: restores to the promisee any benefit he conferred to the promisor.

4. Expectation damages are the difference between promised performance and actual performance—for instance, between a perfect hand and a hairy, scarred hand. *Hawkins v. McGee*.

---

[10] Casebook p. 186.

5. Damages compensate a party for actual losses. No punitive damages. *U.S. Naval Inst. v. Charter Commc'ns, Inc.*

6. Classical contract law did not permit a seller to profit from breach. *Coppola Enters., Inc. v. Alfone*. Some courts viewed it as a breach of the covenant of good faith and fair dealing. *Greer Props., Inc. v. LaSalle Nat'l Bank*.

7. Posner argues for efficient breach. Eisenberg responds that efficient breach is ultimately not so efficient.

8. **Resale paradigm**: A agrees to sell 100,000 widgets to B at $1 a piece. After A delivers 10,000 widgets, C says he desperately needs 25,000 widgets, and he's willing to pay $2 a piece. A agrees to sell to C. He makes a $1,250 profit on C's order, but it delays B's order, causing B $1,000 in damages. But even after paying expectation damages to B, A's breach still earned a profit of $250.[11]

### 2.3.2 Expectation Damages

1. **Breach of contract to perform services**:

    (a) Two remedies: **cost of completion** and **diminution in value**.

    (b) If a contractor leaves a job unfinished, the client can recover **cost of completion** damages. *Louise Caroline Nursing Home, Inc. v. Dix Construction Co.*

    (c) **Builder's damages for the owner's breach**:

    i. The amount the owner owes the builder = (builder's expenditures incurred prior to the breach) + (lost profits) - (amount the owner paid prior to breach).

    ii. Example: A hires B to build a $500,000 house. B spent $400,000 on labor and materials, but the owner only paid $200,000 before breaching. B had no lost profits.

    A. A owes B expenditures ($400,000) + lost profits ($0) - amount paid prior to the breach ($200,000), or **$200,000**.

    (d) **Owner's damages for builder's breach**:

    i. The amount the builder owes the owner = (total cost of completion) - (total original contract price - amount the owner already paid builder).

    ii. Example: A hires B to build a $500,000 house. A pays the full $500,000 up front. B stops halfway through. B did $200,000 worth of work. It will cost $300,000 to finish the job.

    A. B owes A the cost of completion ($300,000) - ($500,000 - $500,000) = **$300,000**.

---

[11] Casebook p. 210.

iii. Example: A hires B to build a $500,000 house. A hasnt paid anything. B stops halfway through. B did $200,000 worth of work. It will cost $300,000 to finish the job.

   A. B owes A the cost of completion ($300,000) - (original contract price ($500,000) - amount already paid ($0)) = -$200,000— i.e., A owes B $200,000.

(e) Where cost of performance exceeds **diminution in value**, courts are likely to award damages only for diminution in value. *Peevyhouse v. Garland Coal & Mining Co.* Courts are wary of awarding cost of completion damages when the cost is **grossly disproportionate** to the benefits (*H.P. Droher & Sons v. Toushin*) or when it would cause **waste** (*Eastern Steamship Lines, Inc. v. United States*).

(f) Courts are more likely to award cost of completion damages when the defects are aesthetically important (e.g., a fancy swimming pool—*City School Dist. of the City of Elmira v. McLane Const. Co.*) or the project involves someone's home (*Fox v. Webb*).

(g) Calculating damages for partially performed services:

   i. Contract price - value of performance completed - amount paid by owner prior to breach. Restatement Second § 346.

   ii. Example: A contracts to build a house for B for $100,000. B breaches halfway through. A would have to spend $60,000 to finish. A's damages are the contract price ($100,000) - cost of completion that the contractor saved ($60,000) = $40,000. A can recover $40,000 minus any payments already made.

2. **Breach of a contract for the sale of goods**:

   (a) The UCC governs.

   (b) **Seller's breach**:

      i. Two remedies: **specific relief** and **damages**.

      ii. UCC § 2-601: if the goods don't match the contract, the buyer can reject, accept, or accept only the commercial parts.

      iii. For defective goods, courts might award damages for the **cost of repair** in excess of the purchase price. UCC § 2-714(2) sets the measure of direct damages for breach of warranty as the difference between the value of the goods as warranted and the value of the goods as accepted, often approximated as the cost of repair.

      iv. When the seller fails to deliver goods sold, the buyer has two options:

         • *Cover*: the buyer purchases a replacement. Damages are the difference between the replacement price and the contract price. UCC § 7-212 and *KGM Harvesting Co. v. Fresh Network*.

- *Hypothetical cover* or **market price** damages: the buyer recovers the difference between the market price at the time of the breach and the contract price. UCC § 7-213.
  v. When covering, the UCC 2-713 allows goods of a different level of quality. *Egerer v. CSR West, LLC.*
  vi. When a buyer covers, can he still recover market price damages under UCC § 7-213, rather than the actual cost of cover under § 2-712?
      - Example: a buyer agrees to buy a steamroller for $1,000. The market price for steamrollers is $1,300 at the time of the breach. The buyer waits six months to cover, when the market price has dropped to $500. Under § 2-712, he can recover nothing, but under 2-713, he can recover $300.
      - The UCC has been updated to force covering buyers to use § 7-212, but most states have not yet adopted the change.
  vii. If replacing the goods is not possible, courts will award the **cost of repair**, even if it exceeds the purchase price. *Continental Sand & Gravel, Inc. v. K & K Sand & Gravel, Inc.*
  viii. Buyers can recover reasonable **incidental damages** related to the goods in question. *Delchi Carrier SpA v. Rotorex Corp.*
(c) **Buyer's breach**:
  i. When buyer breaches and the seller justifiably withholds goods, UCC § 2-718 allows the buyer to win restitution by the amount his payments (i.e., security deposit) exceed (1) specified liquidated damages or (2) 20% of the total performance, or $500, whichever is smaller.
      A. However, the buyer's restitution damages can be offset if the seller shows damages under another UCC provision—e.g., **lost profits** under UCC § 2-708. *Neri v. Retail Marine Corp.*
  ii. A **lost volume seller** has "the capacity to supply the breached units in addition to what it actually sold." Lost volume sellers should be able to recover lost profits from the loss of a single sale. An exception occurs when the volume would be so high that sales would no longer be profitable (e.g., McDonalds can sell a billion hamburgers, but it could not sell 1.5 billion without significant infrastructure expansions—so, the extra 0.5 billion sales would not have been profitable, so McDonalds should not be able to recover for lost sales, even though it is a lost volume seller.) *R.E. Davis Chemical Corp. v. Diasonics, Inc.*
      A. Second-hand car dealers are not lost volume sellers because each used car is unique. If a buyer of a used car breaches, the seller cannot recover if it sells the same car to another buyer for the same price. *Lazenby Garages Ltd. v. Wright.*

3. **Mitigation and contracts for employment**:

    (a) Both parties have a **duty to mitigate** damages after breach. *Rockingham County v. Luten Bridge Co.*

    (b) The duty to mitigate applies even if the goods are different than what the contract specified. *Maden v. Murray & Sons, Inc.*

    (c) The defaulting party cannot dictate how the other party must mitigate. As long as the mitigating party acted **reasonably**, he has fulfilled his duty to mitigate. *In Re Kellet Aircraft Corporation.* Similarly, the mitigating party need not make unreasonable effort to mitigate. *Bank One, Texas N.A. v. Taylor.*

    (d) Where the defendant had an equal opportunity to mitigate loss, he cannot reasonably contend that the plaintiff failed to mitigate. *S.J. Groves & Sons Co. v. Warner Co.*

    (e) Employees have a duty to mitigate, but only by seeking **similar employment**. *Shirley MacLaine Parker v. Twentieth Century-Fox Film Corp., Punkar v. King Plastic Corp.* Employers must compensate wrongfully discharged employees for reasonable expenses incurred in mitigation. *Punkar v. King Plastic Corp.*

    (f) Plaintiffs can recover **reputation damages** if they can prove specific losses. *Redgrave v. Boston Symphony Orchestra, Inc.*[12]

    (g) English courts have allowed recovery for loss of opportunity to appear before the public, but American courts have not, absent evidence of specific losses.

4. **Foreseeability**:

    (a) *Hadley v. Baxendale*:

    i. *First rule*: the party in breach is liable for reasonably foreseeable damages.

    ii. *Second rule*: if the party in breach is aware of special circumstances, he is liable for extra loss those circumstances create. But he is not liable for the extra loss if he was not aware of the special circumstances.

    iii. Courts apply *Hadley* to determine whether a **type** or **amount** of damages is reasonably foreseeable.

    iv. Courts sometimes deviate from the *Hadley* foreseeability rule.[13]

    (b) A commercial machine has only commercial uses. It's reasonably foreseeable that failing to deliver the machine will hinder commerce. *Victoria Laundry (Windsor) Ltd. v. Newman Indus. Ltd.*

---

[12]Squibbed on casebook pp. 276–77.
[13]Casebook pp. 288–89.

(c) Fluctuations in market price are foreseeable. So, for instance, shippers are liable if their delay causes goods to be sold at a lower market price. *Koufos v. C. Czarnikow, Ltd. (The Heron II)*.

(d) If shipments of commercial machinery are delayed, the shipper can be liable for rental charges in the interim, as long as the equipment has an obvious commercial use. *Hector Martinez & Co. v. Southern Pacific Transp. Co.*

5. **Certainty**:

    (a) To recover damages for lost profits, the plaintiff must show with certainty that the breach caused the alleged amount of loss. *Kenford Co. v. Erie County, Ashland Management Inc. v. Janien*.

    (b) The certainty rule has less punch today because we're better at calculating damages.

    (c) The **new business rule**: courts are wary of awarding speculative damages to new ventures.

    (d) Consistency in earlier performance can strengthen the case for speculative damages.

    (e) Statistical evidence of the performance of similar ventures can help establish damages. *Contemporary Mission, Inc. v. Famous Music Corp.*

    (f) **All or nothing rule**: one premise of *Kenford* is that there is some level of certainty above which the plaintiff can fully recover, and below which the plaintiff can recover nothing. This is wrong—the plaintiff should be compensated for the value of the *chance* to earn a profit, even if it is not certain that a profit would result.

    (g) Fuller and Eisenberg propose a formula for calculating damages based on probability based on the Capital Asset Pricing Model: damages should be awarded in proportion their likelihood. So if a venture has as 10% chance of $20 million and a 90% chance of $10 million, the award should be (0.10 x $20 million) + (0.90 x $10 million), or $11 million.

6. **Liquidated damages**:

    (a) Liquidated damages clauses must reasonably approximate anticipated or actual damages. *Wasserman's Inc. v. Middletown*.

    (b) Liquidates damages were traditionally frowned upon because they could be punitive. But today, there's a resurgence, especially among law and economics scholars, because the parties are in the best position to calculate damages.

    (c) Underliquidated damages—an amount less than actual estimated damages—are usually enforced.

(d) Other techniques include limiting liability for consequential damages or provisions that sellers' responsibilities are limited to replacing or repairing defective goods.

### 2.3.3 Specific Performance

1. At common law, only equity courts could award specific performance.

2. Courts will rarely award specific performance when money damages will suffice. *London Bucket Co. v. Stewart*. For efficiency reasons, other courts are willing to award injunctions when damages would be sufficient—e.g., to encourage negotiation. *Walgreen Co. v. Sara Creek Property Co.*

3. Contracts cannot provide for injunctions because the court has sole discretion in determining whether to issue an injunction. *Stokes v. Moore*.

4. Specific performance is appropriate when the **value of property is uncertain, but not because the property is unique**—because every piece of property is unique. *Van Wagner Advertising Corp. v. S & M Enterprises*.

### 2.3.4 Reliance Damages

1. Reliance damages **compensate a party for costs incurred**.

2. When there are **no measurable lost profits**, reliance damages may be the only way to avoid injustice. *Security Stove & Mfg. Co. v. American Rys. Express Co.* Lost potential profits cannot be calculated with certainty, but expenditures can—so when lost profits are uncertain, reliance damages can be appropriate. *Beefy Trail, Inc. v. Beefy King Int'l, Inc.*

3. Expenses made before the contract can be recovered under reliance damages if the breach caused them to be **wasted**. *Anglia Television Co. v. Reed*.

4. Reliance damages should be offset if the seller can prove that the buyer's venture would not have been profitable enough to cover its expenses. *L. Albert & Son v. Armstrong Rubber Co.*

5. A promisee can recover reliance damages from a promisor after the promise was made, but not for similar activity prior to the promise. For instance, as part of a contract with B, C ships goods to A. After several shipments, B defaults. A promises that it will pay C for the goods it ships to A. C can recover reliance damages for the cost of shipments after A's promise, but not for prior shipments. *Westside Galvanizing Servs., Inc. v. Georgia-Pacific Corp.*

### 2.3.5 Restitution Damages

1. The non-breaching party will sometimes be satisfied with rescission of the contract and restitution of any value conferred on the breaching party. The purpose of restitution is to **prevent unjust enrichment**. *Osteen v. Johnson.*

2. Restitution damages are based on **benefit incurred**. while reliance damages are based on **cost incurred**.

3. **Unjust enrichment**: measured by the benefit the plaintiff conferred on the defendant.

4. *Quantum meruit*: measured by the value of the plaintiff's services. The plaintiff can recover even if performance of the contract would have resulted in a loss. *United States v. Algernon Blair, Inc.*

5. **Restitution vs. quantum meruit**—bank error in your favor:

    (a) Restitution: you have to give the money back. Otherwise, you'd be unjustly enriched.

    (b) Quantum meruit: the bank can recover nothing because it did not render any service of value.

6. Restitution damages are not available when parties have performed all of the contract except payment. *Oliver v. Campbell.*

7. The promisee in an unprofitable contract can recover the value of benefit incurred, even if it exceeds the contract price. *United States v. Algernon Blair, Inc.* For costs incurred (i.e., reliance damages), the damages award should not exceed the contract price.

    (a) Restatement § 349: reliance damages are an alternative to expectation damages—but they should only apply when expectation damages are too uncertain or should be limited for other reasons.

8. At common law, the breaching party could not recover. However, the modern trend is to **allow the breaching party to recover for benefit conferred** (minus actual injuries). To allow the non-breaching party to retain the benefit conferred beyond actual injury would be unjust enrichment. *Kutzin v. Pirnie*, Restatement § 374(1).

    (a) " . . . the breaching party is entitled to the reasonable value of its services less any damages caused by the breach."[14]

    (b) " . . . a party injured by breach of contract is entitled to retain nothing in excess of that sum which compensates him for the loss of his bargain."[15] *Vines v. Orchard Hills, Inc.*

---

[14] Casebook p. 362.
[15] Casebook p. 364.

## 2.4 Assent

### 2.4.1 Interpretation

1. **Subjectivity and objectivity**:

    (a) Contracts generally require a **"meeting of the minds."**[16]

    (b) What happens in cases of misinterpretation? There's a tension between subjective and objective intent.

    (c) Courts will hold parties to a party's "outward expression as expressing his intent, rather than his "secret and unexpressed intention."[17] *Lucy v. Zehmer.*

    (d) No contract is made when "the whole transaction between the parties was a frolic and a banter."[18] *Keller v. Holderman.*

    (e) If there are **"latent ambiguities"** (e.g., multiple ships named "Peerless"), courts will accept additional evidence of the parties' intent. If there was no meeting of the minds, there was no contract. *Raffles v. Wichelhaus, Oswald v. Allen.*

    i. "If neither party can be assigned the greater blame for the misunderstanding, there is no nonarbitrary basis for deciding which party's understanding to enforce, so the parties are allowed to abandon the contract without liability."[19] *Colfax Envelope Corp. v. Local No. 458-3M.*

    (f) Courts consider many sources in determining the meaning of a word, including dictionaries, trade usage, regulatory usage, and plain meaning. *Frigaliment Importing Co. v. B.N.S. Intern. Sales Co.*

    (g) Parties can communicate in codes unique to them as long as both parties agree on the meaning. *Falck v. Williams.*

    (h) Contracts generally require a meeting of the minds, but intent is irrelevant if the other party **could not reasonably know** the other's intent (and if the objective meaning was clear). *Embry v. Hargadine, McKittrick Dry Goods Co.*

    (i) If one party knows the other's subjective intent, he can't fool him by making an agreement that intentionally contradicts that intent (e.g., if a buyer thinks he's buying unencumbered property, the seller can't conceal the current tenant's purchase option). *Mayol v. Weiner Companies, Ltd.*

    (j) **Classical vs. modern interpretation**:

    i. Classical contract law largely **disregarded the parties' intent**.

---

[16] Casebook p. 368.
[17] Casebook p. 373.
[18] Casebook p. 374.
[19] Casebook p. 381.

ii. There are **four principles of interpretation** in modern contract law:[20]

   A. The more reasonable meaning prevails. If both parties attach different subjective meanings to an expression and they are not equally reasonable.

   B. But if the two meanings are equally reasonable, neither prevails.

   C. If the parties attach the same meaning, that meaning prevails even if it is unreasonable.

   D. If A and B attach different meanings, and A knows B's meaning but B doesn't know A's, B's meaning prevails even if it is less reasonable.

(k) " . . . where the parties have not clearly expressed the **duration of a contract**, the courts will imply that they intended performance to continue for a reasonable time."[21]

2. **Problems of interpretation:**

   (a) Some courts hold that they should take **"material circumstances"** into account to honor the parties' intent. *Spaulding v. Morse*. Others disagree. *Lawson v. Martin Timber Co.*

   (b) Some amount of interpretation is always necessary—e.g., "fetch some soupmeat."[22]

3. **Trade usage**:

   (a) **Trade usage** applies to terms of agreements between parties involved in a particular trade, e.g., textiles. *Foxco Industries, Ltd. v. Fabric World, Inc.*

      i. **Trade quantities** can vary if the usage is customary within the trade—e.g., 4,000 shingles can really mean 2,500. *Hurst v. W.J. Lake & Co.*

      ii. If one party is unaware of the trade usage, but should have known, there is a fundamental difference in intent and thus no contract. *Flower City Painting Contractors, Inc. v. Gumina* (following *Raffles v. Wichelhaus*).

## 2.4.2 Offer and Revocation

1. Key concepts: **intent, clarity, revocation.**

2. **What constitutes an offer?**

---

[20] Casebook p. 394–95.
[21] Casebook p. 401.
[22] Casebook p. 405.

(a) **Negotiation vs. firm offer**: there is an important distinction between intent to find out if the other party is interested and intent to make a definite offer. *Lonergan v. Scolnick.*

(b) If a party reserves the right to not accept an offer, a proposal is only an **invitation** to submit an offer. *Regent Lighting Corp. v. CMT Corp.*

(c) **Unilateral offer**: a binding obligation arises from newspaper ads if "the facts show that some performance was promised in positive terms for something requested."[23] " . . . where the offer is **clear, definite, and explicit**, and leaves nothing open for negotiation, it constitutes an offer, acceptance of which will complete the contract."[24] *Lefkowitz v. Great Minneapolis Surplus Store.*

   i. But, courts have imposed limits—e.g., an ad offering 11% financing on a car does not constitute an offer because not everyone will qualify for that rate. *Ford Motor Credit Co. v. Russell.*

   ii. Is a newspaper ad an offer or an invitation to negotiate? Courts generally hold that it is an offer if it **requires the consumer to perform a specific act** (e.g., first come, first served). But does that align with consumers' reasonable expectations? Does traveling to the store count as an act? *Donovan v. RRL Corp.*

   iii. Displaying something in a shop window with a price tag is an invitation, not an offer. *Fisher v. Bell.*

(d) People are not legally bound when they make appointments or reservations.[25]

3. **Lapse, rejection, and counteroffer**:

   (a) "An offer may be **terminated** in a number of ways, as, for example, where it is **rejected** by the offeree, or where it is not accepted by him within the **time fixed**, or, if no time is fixed, within a **reasonable time**. An offer terminated in either of these ways ceases to exist and cannot therefore be accepted."[26] *Akers v. J.B. Sedberry, Inc.*

   (b) A **qualified acceptance**, subject to a condition, does not create a contractual obligation if the other party does not satisfy the condition—e.g., offering to buy a house only if the previous owners left behind the furniture. *Ardente v. Horan.*

      i. If the conditional acceptance does not add any conditions to the contract, but rather releases the offeror from an obligation, it is an ordinary binding acceptance (not a conditional acceptance)—e.g., buying land from a railroad but relieving the railroad from

---

[23] Williston. Casebook p. 418.
[24] Casebook p. 419.
[25] Casebook p. 424.
[26] Casebook p. 427.

its obligation to remove tracks from the land. *Rhode Island Dep't of Transp. v. Providence & Worcester R.R.*

    ii. A grumbling acceptance is still an acceptance. "The notation amounted to no more than saying I don't like your offer, I don't think it's right or fair, but I accept it. That and nothing more."[27] *Price v. Oklahoma College of Osteopathic Medicine and Surgery.*

    iii. The condition is not part of the offer if the offeree's acceptance does not depend on the condition—e.g., renewing a lease with a request to build a cookroom. *Culton v. Gilchrist.*

(c) Under classical contract law, the **mirror image rule** held that no contract was formed if the acceptance differed from the offer in any way. Modern contract law has softened the rule in two ways:

    i. UCC § 2-207—see below (battle of the forms).

    ii. Restatement Second § 59: an acceptance containing additional terms is binding if acceptance does not depend on the offeror's assent to the additional terms.

(d) A seller can **renew an offer by implication**. *Livingstone v. Evans.*

    i. For instance—S: I'll sell for $1,800. B: How about $1,600? S: Sorry, can't go any lower. B: Ok, then, $1,800.

    ii. S renewed the offer by implication.

(e) If the offeror **dies or becomes incapacitated**, and the offeree is unaware, then classical contract law holds that the offeror's estate is bound. Some modern courts have criticized the rule as out of step with the parties' intent. Eisenberg proposes that the offeree be able to recover reliance damages but not expectation damages.[28]

(f) **Receipt** happens when the person conducting the transaction receives it or "when it would have been brought to his attention if the organization had exercised due diligence . . . ."[29]

4. **Revocation**:

(a) Under classical contract law, the **unilateral contract rule** held that an offer "could be revoked at any time before the designated act had been completed, even if performance of the act had begun."[30]

    i. This rule frustrated the parties' expectations and defied the interests of offerors as a class.[31]

    ii. So, the Restatement (First) drew a distinction between **performing** and **preparing to perform**, which the court followed in *Ragosta v. Wilder*. But the distinction can be hard to justify.

---

[27] Casebook p. 435.
[28] Casebook pp. 437–38.
[29] Casebook p. 442.
[30] Casebook p. 446.
[31] Casebook pp. 446–47.

For instance, say the unilateral offer is that I'll give you $1,000 to cross the Brooklyn Bridge. If you take one step on the bridge, there is a contract. But if you spend hours preparing, there is no contract.

(b) Common law: "an offer is **freely revocable**, even if the offeror has promised to hold it open, unless that promise is supported by **consideration or reliance**."[32] See *Ragosta v. Wilder*. But there have been recent changes:

  i. UCC: merchants can make a "firm offer" (i.e., an irrevocable offer) without the need for consideration. The offeror must be a merchant, etc.[33]

  ii. CISG Art. 16 allows an offeror to make an irrevocable offer without these restrictions.

(c) **Promissory estoppel prevents a subcontractor from revoking its offer** once the contractor has acted upon the subcontractor's promise. *Drennan v. Star Paving Co.*

  i. **Asymmetry**: subcontractors are bound to the general, but the general is not bound to the subcontractor, creating incentives for the general contractor to act unethically:

   A. *Bid shopping*: using the lowest bid to negotiate lower bids from others.

   B. *Bid chopping*: pressuring the subcontractor to make a lower bid.

   C. *Bid peddling*: a subcontractor waits until other bids are in and then undercutting them, avoiding the cost of estimating his own bid.

  ii. Most courts have followed *Drennan*, but at least one has deviated.[34]

  iii. § 90 reliance damages may not be available when the general contractor engages in these kinds of unethical practices. *Preload Technology, Inc. v. A.B. & J. Construction Co., Inc.*

(d) **Option contracts**:

  i. An option contract is an offer in which the offeror promises to keep the offer open for a certain period of time. For instance, a seller grants a buyer the option to buy his house for $1,000 anytime during the next month.

  ii. "An offer which the offeror should reasonably expect to induce action or forbearance of a substantial character on the part of the offence before acceptance and which does induce such action or forbearance is binding as an option contract to the extent necessary to avoid injustice."

---

[32] Casebook p. 453.
[33] Casebook p. 453.
[34] Casebook p. 453.

iii. The distinction between §§ 45 (creating a binding option contract when the offeree begins to perform) and 87 is that an offeree who has begun performance can recover expectation damages, while an offeree who has not begun performance can only recover reliance damages.[35]

### 2.4.3 Modes of Acceptance

1. The offeror is the master of his offer. He can specify a mode of acceptance.

2. **Acceptance by act**:

    (a) A promise becomes binding when the offeree acts on the offeror's request—e.g., if you promise to devise your property to someone if he takes care of you, his acts of care count as acceptance. *Klockner v. Green*.

    (b) "So long as the outstanding offer was known to him, a person may accept an offer for a unilateral contract by rendering performance, even if he does so primarily for **reasons unrelated to the offer**"[36]—e.g., going on an ordinary fishing trip and catching Diamond Jim III. *Simmons v. United States*.

    (c) Payment of rewards shouldn't be based on knowledge of the reward. Do we want people to avoid doing their civic duty unless they know they'll get paid? *Stephens v. Memphis*.

    (d) **Performing a condition counts as acceptance of the offer.** For instance, if the Carbolic Smoke Ball manufacturers promise a reward for anyone who uses the product and gets sick, anyone who performs those conditions has accepted the offer and can recover the reward. *Carlill v. Carbolic Smoke Ball, Inc.*

3. **Subjective acceptance:**

    (a) Notice of acceptance is distinct from acceptance itself. If notice is not required, subjective acceptance counts as acceptance to make the offer binding. *International Filter Co. v. Conroe Gin, Ince, & Light Co.*

4. **Acceptance by conduct:**

    (a) **Regular conduct** can count as tacit assent to contractual terms. "... when an offeree accepts the offeror's services without expressing any objections to the offer's essential terms, the offeree has manifested assent to those terms."[37] *Polaroid Corp. v. Rollins Environmental Services (NJ), Inc.*

---

[35] Casebook p. 455.
[36] Casebook p. 466.
[37] Casebook p. 478.

5. **The effect of using a subcontractor's bid**:

    (a) If a general contractor uses a subcontractor's bid in submitting its own bid, it is not bound to use the subcontractor's services. There are several justifications for "unequal treatment of generals and subcontractors . . . "[38] *Holman Erection Co. v. Orville E. Madsen & Sons, Inc.*

        i. The statute underlying *Holman* was later amended to prevent general contractors from substituting subcontractors unless the subcontractor was unable or unwilling to perform.[39]

6. **Silence as acceptance**:

    (a) By default, **silence does not constitute acceptance**. *Vogt v. Madden.*

    (b) Restatement Second § 69 recognizes **two exceptions**: (1) when the offeree **silently takes offered benefits** and (2) "where one party **relies** on the other party's manifestation of intention that silence may operate as acceptance."[40]

    (c) "Where the offeree with reasonable opportunity to reject offered services **takes the benefit** of them under circumstances which would indicate to a reasonable person that they were offered with the expectation of compensation, he assents to the term proposed and thus accepts the offer."[41] *Laurel Race Courses v. Regal Const. Co.*

    (d) Delay in rejection can count as acceptance. "It will not do to say that a seller of goods like these could wait indefinitely to decide whether or not he will accept the offer of the proposed buyer."[42] *Cole-McIntyre-Norfleet Co. v. Holloway.* In some cases, there is a duty to promptly reply, and unreasonable delay will count as acceptance—e.g., a hail insurer waiting two months to send a rejection. *Kukusa v. Home Mut. Hail-Tornado Ins. Co.*

    (e) Repeated orders for the same product can count as a **standing offer**. If the buyer does not reject future shipments, his silence counts as acceptance. *Hobbs v. Massasoit Whip Co.*

    (f) Taking physical control of shipped goods counts as acceptance of the shipment. *Louisville Tin & Stove Co. v. Lay.*

    (g) If you enjoy the benefit of an unwanted thing, you have to pay for it—e.g., an expired newspaper subscription. *Austin v. Burge.*

---

[38] Casebook p. 483.
[39] Casebook p. 485.
[40] Casebook p. 493.
[41] Casebook p. 495.
[42] Casebook p. 497.

(h) A **negative-option** plan involves a subscription for merchandise, like a book or record club. They differ from unordered goods in that the customer contracts in advance. Silence indicates continued acceptance.

7. **Acceptance by electronic agent**:

    (a) VETA and E-Sign have clarified that electronic records and signatures satisfy the statute of frauds.

    (b) Contracts can be formed between a person and a computer, or even between two computers.[43] " ... it is conceivable that, with the useful life of this Act, electronic agents may be created with the ability to act autonomously, and not just automatically."[44]

### 2.4.4 Implied-in-Law and Implied-in-Fact Contracts

1. **Implied-in-fact** contracts are true contracts in which assent is implied, not explicit—e.g., raising your hand to bid at an auction.[45]

2. **Implied-in-law** contracts aren't really contracts. There's no offer, acceptance, or assent. But to prevent unjust enrichment, someone should be rewarded.

3. "Contracts implied in law, or as they are more commonly called 'quasi contracts,' are obligations imposed by law on grounds of justice and equity. Their purpose is to **prevent unjust enrichment**. Unlike express contracts or contracts implied in fact, quasi contracts do not rest upon the assent of the contracting parties."[46]

    (a) The **officious intermeddler** doctrine prevents foisting labor upon another without consent. But the **emergency aid exception** allows recovery if the intervener "acted unofficiously and with intent to charge"[47]—for instance, medically necessary nursing services that the patient did not consent to. *Nursing Care Services, Inc. v. Dobos*

4. Implied-in-fact contracts: the *parties* decide that there is a contract. Implied-in-law: the *court* decides.

5. When someone else confers value on you, and you know he expects payment, your silence is assent to pay (i.e., the court will find a contract implied in law—otherwise you'd be unjustly enriched). *Day v. Caton*.

6. Damages vary:[48]

---

[43] Casebook p. 502.
[44] Casebook p. 503.
[45] Casebook p. 508.
[46] Casebook p. 505.
[47] Casebook p. 505.
[48] Casebook p. 515.

(a) Implied-in-fact contracts are based on the parties' intentions, so the proper remedy is compensatory damages.

(b) Implied-in-law contracts are based on unjust enrichment, so the proper remedy is the value of the benefit acquired.

(c) Damages in an unjust enrichment (i.e., implied in law) claim are measured by the benefit conferred. Damages in a quantum meruit claim are measured by the reasonable value of the plaintiff's services.[49]

7. **Employee handbooks**:

    (a) Provisions in employee handbooks are enforceable. *Pine River State Bank v. Mettille.*

    (b) What happens if the employer modifies the handbook and the employee continues to work? Does the employee's continued work constitute acceptance of the modification? Courts are split.[50] Courts are also split on whether to enforce disclaimers.[51]

### 2.4.5 Preliminary Negotiations, Indefiniteness, and the Duty to Bargain in Good Faith

1. Agreements can be **too indefinite** to allow courts to fashion remedies for breach, and are therefore unenforceable.

    (a) There is no contract if the parties lack a mutual understanding of the essential parts of the agreement. The court cannot substitute the missing terms if they are central to the contract. *Academy Chicago Publishers v. Cheever.*

    (b) "An agreement to enter into an agreement upon terms to be afterwards settled between the parties is a contradiction in terms."[52] *Ridgway v. Wharton.*

    (c) If the essential parts of an agreement are included and agreed upon, the contract is enforceable even if other clauses are omitted.[53] *Bery Agency v. Sleepworld-Willingboro, Inc.* Courts should **fill gaps** where the parties' reasonable expectations are clear, but they should not impose performance to which the party would not have agreed. *Rego v. Decker.*

    (d) Parties may want to create incomplete contracts to allow future flexibility. *AROK Construction Co. v. Indian Construction Services.*

    (e) There is a general understanding in the trade that subcontractors will enter into an agreement with the general contractor after submitting

---

[49] Casebook pp. 515–16.
[50] Casebook pp. 531–33.
[51] Casebook pp. 533–34.
[52] Casebook p. 541.
[53] Casebook p. 541.

a winning bid, even if it contained no terms other than the price. If this were not the case, general contractors would be unable to recover § 90 reliance damages. *Saliba-Kringlen Corp. v. Allen Engineering Co.*

(f) The UCC "gap-filler" provisions fill the gaps that parties may leave in contracts for sale of goods.

  i. **Default rules**: background rules that the law reads into a contract only if the parties left them out.
  
  ii. **Mandatory rules**: not waivable by the parties, e.g., the requirement of consideration. If the parties leave them out, there is no contract.

(g) If there is no method in a lease for calculating rent, the court cannot determine that the parties intended to be bound by fair market value. *Joseph Martin, Jr., Delicatessen, Inc. v. Schumacher.* But some courts, applying a minority rule, find that the parties at least would have intended rent to be "reasonable." *Moolenaar v. Co-Build Companies, Inc.*

2. **Offer and acceptance** vs. **preliminary negotiations**:

    (a) Classical contract law drew a strict binary distinction between offer and acceptance, which created a binding agreement, and preliminary negotiations, which did not.[54]

3. What about agreements to create **future agreements**? Again classical contract law followed a strict binary: on the one hand, if the future agreement was meant only to confirm the original agreement, the original agreement was enforceable; on the other hand, if the parties intended not to be bound unless they executed the future agreement, the original agreement was not enforceable.

4. Classical contract law recognized no duty to negotiate in good faith,[55] though the parties themselves could agree to good faith negotiations.[56] *Channel Home Centers v. Grossman.*

### 2.4.6 Parol Evidence

1. Thayer: some want a "lawyer's Paradise" where written instruments have a precise, fixed meaning. But in reality, context is a "fatal necessity."[57]

2. Should we allow oral evidence or require the parties to put their entire agreement in formal, written terms? Williston would exclude oral evidence unless similarly situated parties would have supplemented the writ-

---

[54] Casebook p. 536.
[55] Casebook p. 537.
[56] Casebook p. 553.
[57] Casebook p. 590.

ten agreement with oral terms. Corbin would allow evidence of intent beyond the writing itself. Corbin has largely won.[58]

3. The classical, Willistonian view: courts should **presume complete integration**, "and should admit evidence of consistent additional terms only if there is substantial evidence that the parties did not intend the writing to embody the entire agreement."[59] *Hatley v. Stafford.*

4. Restatement Second § 209 determines whether an agreement is integrated as "a question of fact to be determined in accordance with all relevant evidence." The Restatement follows Corbin, who argued that on this issue, "no relevant testimony should be excluded."[60]

5. If the parties might reasonably have left terms out of the agreement, the court can admit evidence of the parties' intent and oral agreements. For instance, in a purchase option agreement, the parties might not have written down a provision that the option was personal to that party and nonassignable. *Masterson v. Sine.*

6. UCC § 2-202 reflects Corbin's influence in its focus on the intent of the parties, rather than the practices of reasonable people. *Interform v. Mitchell Constr. Co.*

7. UCC § 2-202 provides that parol evidence may explain or supplement a written agreement agreement, but not contradict it. According to the court, a term is inconsistent if it contradicts or negates a term of the writing. If it does not, it is admissible. *Hunt Foods and Industries, Inc. v. Doliner.*

    (a) The *Hunt Foods* view of consistency is too narrow. A better definition is "the absence of reasonable harmony in terms of the language and respective obligations of the parties."[61] *Alaska Northern Development, Inc. v. Alyeska Pipeline Service Co.*

8. **Merger (or integration) clauses** provide that the written contract is the entire agreement between the parties.[62]

    (a) Under classical contract law, courts presume complete integration.

    (b) Today, a merger clause is often not enough to prove complete integration. Courts often hold that the parties must have actually assented to integration.

---

[58]Casebook p. 592. On Corbin's greater influence, see *Interform Co. v. Mitchell Constr. Co.*, p. 594.
[59]Casebook p. 594.
[60]Casebook p. 595.
[61]Casebook p. 601.
[62]Casebook p. 602.

(c) Courts must consider surrounding circumstances to determine whether the parties actually assented to the merger clause. *ARB (American Research Bureau), Inc. v. E-Systems, Inc.*

(d) UCC § 2-202 requires intent to integrate in addition to a merger clause. In a written contract, the merger clause must be conspicuous. *Siebel v. Layne & Bowler, Inc.*

9. **Fraud exception**: otherwise inadmissible parol evidence is admissible if it shows an "invalidating cause" of the written agreement—e.g., lack of consideration, duress, mistake, illegality, or fraud.[63]

10. **Condition-to-legal-effectiveness exception**:

    (a) The parol evidence rule does not apply when the occurrence or nonoccurence of an event, by spoken agreement, is a condition to making the written agreement binding or effective.[64]

    (b) For instance, A and B make a written business agreement, and agree orally that the agreement will be null if the parties fail to raise $600,000 within 20 days. Evidence of the oral agreement is admissible.

11. The parol evidence rule applies only to oral agreements made **before or contemporaneously with a written, integrated contract**. The rule doesn't apply to a later agreement that modifies the integration.[65]

12. Written contracts often provide that they can be modified only in writing—a private Statute of Frauds. These are **no oral modification (n.o.m.)** clauses.

    (a) Common law: oral modifications are enforceable notwithstanding n.o.m. clauses, because the later oral agreement by implication modifies the earlier written agreement containing the n.o.m. clause.

    (b) Example: "I'll pay you $100 to lock me in this room. Don't let me out for 10 hours, no matter what I say." You sign the agreement. At common law, cries of "I changed my mind, I'll pay you $500 to let me out!" would modify the original agreement.

    (c) UCC § 2-209 makes two key changes to the common law:

        i. § 2-209(1): a modification needs no consideration to be enforceable.

        ii. § 2-209(2): if a contract for the sale of goods contains a n.o.m. clause, the modification must be in writing.

---

[63] Casebook p. 604.
[64] Casebook p. 606.
[65] Casebook p. 208.

(d) But, § 2-209(4) allows that an attempt at modification under § 2-209(2) can operate as a waiver. But then § 2-209(5) provides that a party who has created a waiver for an executory (unperformed) part of the contract can retract it if the other party has relied on the waiver.

### 2.4.7 Plain Meaning

1. "... where language is clear and unambiguous, the focus of interpretation is upon the terms of the agreement as *manifestly* expressed, rather than as, perhaps, silently intended."[66] *Steuart v. McChesney*.

2. Some courts hold that the judge's linguistic reference point is necessarily different than the parties'. Parties should be allowed to introduce reasonable alternative interpretations of the written agreement. *Mellon Bank, N.A. v. Aetna Business Credit, Inc.*.

3. UCC § 2-202 assumes that the written contract is not completely integrated. Under the UCC, the court should admit parole evidence by default unless the judge thinks the written agreement is unambiguous.

4. Traynor vs. Kozinski:

   (a) Language lacks fixed meaning. "Accordingly, rational interpretation requires at least a preliminary consideration of all credible evidence offered to prove the intention of the parties."[67] Traynor in *Pacific Gas & Electric Co. v. G.W. Thomas Drayage & Rigging Co.*

   (b) There are some cases where the plain meaning of language really is unambiguous. Kozinski grudgingly agreed that the external evidence must be allowed under the California Supreme Court's holding in *Pacific Gas*—which "we have no difficulty understanding..., even without extrinsic evidence to guide us."[68] Kozinski in *Trident Center v. Connecticut General Life Ins. Co.*

   (c) What exactly wrong with following the *PG&E* rule? If the language is in fact unambiguous, the case will easily fall at trial. The only cost is judicial inefficiency, which is costly in terms of time and money, but not analytically.

## 2.5 Form Contracts

1. **Battle of the forms and UCC § 2-207:**

---

[66] Casebook p. 608.
[67] Casebook p. 617.
[68] Casebook p. 621.

(a) **Battle of the forms**: buyers and sellers exchange elaborate preprinted form contracts. It would be prohibitively costly for buyers to actually read the contracts—**rational ignorance**.[69]

(b) The **last shot** rule: under classical contract law, conduct can constitute acceptance—e.g., the buyer could tacitly accept the terms of the deal by accepting and keeping the goods. In that case, the last form the parties exchanged would control.[70]

(c) UCC § 2-204: general formation of a contract.

(d) UCC § 2-207: there can be a contract even if the language of the forms differs. The conflicting language is removed and, if necessary, replaced with gap-fillers. It rejects the mirror image rule.

   i. The premise behind § 2-207 is that no rational person reads the boilerplate terms.

(e) § 2-207 does not apply to **non-form, fully negotiated** agreements. "Under such circumstances, when the parties fully negotiate each provision of a contract, a contract may be 'beyond the reach of 2-207 and adrift on the murky sea of common law.'"[71] *Columbia Hyundai, Inc. v. Carll Hyundai, Inc.*

(f) When does a response become **"expressly conditional,"** making it a counteroffer for purposes of § 2-207? If the dickered terms are identical but the undickered terms vary, the transaction does not become "expressly conditional" and the response does not become a counteroffer. *Gardner Zemke Co. v. Dunham Bush, Inc.*

   i. Courts are split on the meaning of "expressly made conditional." Some hold that that if acceptance is "expressly made conditional," it must be "directly and distinctly stated."[72] Others apply looser standards, e.g., requiring certain key phrases, or requiring the offeree to demonstrate unwillingness to proceed unless he agrees to the additional terms.

(g) **Knockout rule**: under 2-207, conflicting terms cancel each other out.

(h) **"Materially alter"** under 2-207(2)(b): a term added in an acceptance does not become part of the contract if it would "materially alter" the contract. The UCC defines "materially alter" to mean "would result in [unreasonable] surprise or hardship." So, for instance, a mandatory arbitration clause is not a material alteration.[73]

2. **Rolling contracts:**

---

[69] Casebook pp. 639–40.
[70] Casebook pp. 641–42.
[71] Casebook p. 644.
[72] Casebook p. 655.
[73] Casebook pp. 653–55.

(a) **"Money now, terms later"**: shrinkwrap agreements, in which a buyer purchases software and must agree to additional license terms before using it, are valid. *ProCD, Inc. v. Zeidenberg*. The rule applies to both software and hardware. *Hill v. Gateway 2000*.

(b) Clickwrap agreements, in which a user must agree to terms before using software, are valid, but they require "[r]easonably conspicuous notice of the existence of contract terms and unambiguous manifestation of assent to those terms by consumers . . ."[74] *Specht v. Netscape Communications Corp.*

3. **Interpretation and unconscionability in form contracts**:

    (a) Reformation is appropriate only if there is mutual mistake. *Sardo v. Fidelity & Deposit Co.*

    (b) Form contracts can be unenforceable on the basis of public policy. *Weaver v. American Oil Co.*

4. Llewellyn on form contracts:

    (a) Form contracts are attractive. But they can take on "a massive and almost terrifying jug-handled character."[75] Nobody really reads them.

    (b) So, nobody really assents to boilerplate terms. Rather, people only really assent to the dickered terms.

    (c) "[A]ny contract with boiler-plate results in *two* several contracts: the *dickered* deal, and the collateral one of *supplementary* boiler-plate."[76]

## 2.6 Mistake and Unexpected Circumstances

1. **Unilateral mistake (mechanical error)**: courts will grant relief if (1) the other party has not relied on the error or (2) reliance damages will not compensate the other party. See the Nolan Ryan baseball card case.

2. **Mistakes in transcription**: if there is proof of an agreement, courts will reform an error in transcription as long as "there has been no prejudicial change of position by the other party while ignorant of the mistake." *Travelers Ins. Co. v. Bailey*. But if the parties purposely based the contract on an uncertain event, there will be no reformation. *Chimart Associates v. Paul*.

3. **Tacit assumptions** are present in every contract—e.g., the sun will rise tomorrow.

---

[74] Casebook p. 686.
[75] Casebook p. 694.
[76] Casebook p. 696.

4. **Mutual mistake**: tacit or explicit assumptions in the agreement turn out to be incorrect.

    (a) The *Sherwood* rule held that a mistake excuses performance when it relates to the "substance" or "root" of the contract, but not if it relates to something peripheral. *Sherwood v. Walker*. But the *Sherwood* rule was all but overruled shortly after. *Nester v. Michigan Land & Iron Co.*

    (b) **Impossibility**: when the parties' mistke renders performance impossible, performance is excused. *Griffith v. Brymer*.

    (c) If there was no fraud and neither party could have known about the mistake, the parties cannot rescind the agreement. *Wood v. Boynton*.

    (d) When the market price of an item depends on collective judgment (e.g., fine art), there is no mistake if the collective judgment later shifts (e.g., the art world discovers that a different artist painted a piece). *Firestone & Parson, Inc. v. Union League of Philadelphia*.

    (e) " . . . rescission is indicated when the mistaken belief relates to a **basic assumption** of the parties upon which the contract is made, and which materially affects the agreed performance of the party." *Lewanee County Board of Health v. Messerly*.

    (f) The buyer's assumption of risk (e.g., through an as-is) clause can enforce performance despite a mistake. But, some courts have held that the buyer's assumption of risk os only relevant when the parties were *aware* of the possibility that they were wrong. *Beachcomber Coins, Inc. v. Boskett*.

5. **Unexpected circumstances**:

    (a) **Implied conditions**: when performance depends on the continued existence of a person or thing, that person or thing is an implied condition. When that person or thing perishes, performance is excused. *Taylor v. Caldwell* (the plaintiff could rescind the contract because a concert hall burned down).

    (b) Contracts involve many **tacit assumptions**. "We 'just know' that the burning of a music hall violates a tacit assumption of the parties who executed a contract for hiring it for a few days; we 'just know' that a two per cent increase in the price of beans does not violate a tacit assumption underlying a contract to deliver a ton of beans for a fixed price."[77]

    (c) **Impracticability**: performance becomes "impossible in legal contemplation" if it is beyond practicality—e.g., retrieving underwater gravel. *Mineral Park Land Co. v. Howard*. But gambling on your own abilities and failing does not count as impracticability—e.g.,

---

[77] Casebook p. 769.

promising to deliver an engineering breakthrough. *United States v. Wegematic Corp.* Bargaining on uncertainty likewise does not invalidate a contract if uncertain term turns out to be unfavorable. *Missouri Public Service Co. v. Peabody Coal Co.*

6. **The duty to perform in good faith:**

    (a) "... in every contract there exists an **implied covenant of good faith and fair dealing**."[78] *Kirke La Shelle Co. v. Paul Armstrong Co.*

    (b) Parties implicitly agree to not interfere with the other's performance. *Patterson v. Meyerhofer.*

    (c) But, "[m]ere difficulty of performance will not excuse a breach of contract"—even if one of the parties contributed to that difficulty by affecting the market. It's ok to interfere with performance indirectly. *Iron Trade Products Co. v. Wilkoff Co.*

    (d) Good faith in the UCC means "honesty in fact and the observance of reasonable commercial standards of fair dealing."[79] Both the UCC and the Restatement (Second) require good faith performance.

    (e) What does "good faith" mean?[80]

        i. Farnsworth: it's a fundamental idea of contract law. It implies terms in the contract.

        ii. Summers: the "excluder" analysis asks, what does a judge want to rule out by use of the phrase "good faith"? It has no meaning on its own, but it serves to exclude many heterogeneous forms of bad faith.

        iii. Burton: the "forgone opportunity analysis" argues that "good faith" limits what a party can do in performance, so bad faith is to "recapture opportunities forgone upon contracting..."

        iv. Courts apply all three standards.

## 2.7 Berring's Basic Rules

1. There are no villains in contract law. (Holmes.)

2. Look at the cold facts. What specifically happened? (Holmes again.)

3. That which is not clear cannot be made clear.

---

[78] Casebook p. 890.
[79] Casebook p. 891.
[80] Casebook pp. 892–93.

# § 3  Introduction

1. Contracts: voluntary obligations—imposed on the basis of a commitment, e.g., a promise. Emphasizes personal autonomy.

2. Torts: involuntary obligations—imposed regardless of prior commitments.

3. "Morality justifies promise-keeping more than law ever will."—Berring.

4. Relational contract theory: contracts involve trust and long-term relationships, rather than just discrete transactions.

5. Spectrum of agreement: Promise → Gift → Contractual Relationship.

6. Contract disputes involve someone trying to get out of an obligation—usually an obligation arising from an agreement that person created. Who wants in and who wants out?

7. Fungible goods are interchangeable with property of the same kind (wheat, corn, money). Nonfungible goods are not (land, your wedding ring).

## 3.1  Rawls, "A Theory of Justice"

1. A person must follow the rules when "he has voluntarily accepted the benefits of the scheme or has taken advantage of the opportunities of offers to advance his interests . . ."[81]

2. Making a promise means accepting the social benefits it brings—e.g., the guarantee that the other person will hold up his end of the bargain. This obligation is self-imposed.

3. " . . . promising is an act done with the public intention of deliberately incurring an obligation the existence of which in the circumstances will further one's ends."[82]

## 3.2  Scanlon, "Promises and Practices"

1. The "Guilty Secret": Harold asks you not to tell a particular embarrassing story about him to his new colleagues. You agree.

2. You now have two moral reasons not to tell the story:

    (a) It would gratuitously hurt Harold.

    (b) It would violate your obligation.

3. Where does your obligation come from?

---

[81] Fuller and Eisenberg, *Basic Contract Law*, 8th Ed., p. 1.
[82] Casebook p. 2.

(a) Harold might have relied in small part on your promise. He didn't get down and beg, for instance. But for the most part, your promise did not affect his conduct.

(b) The promise itself has inherent value. First, it gives Harold peace of mind. More importantly, Harold has a reason for wanting the assurance, and you have reasons for giving it.

4. **"Principle F"** describes the mutual obligations between the promisor and promisee.[83]

5. In "Principle F" cases, (1) it would be wrong for the promisor not to perform, and (2) the promisee has a right to rely on performance and a right to enforce if the other party breaks the promise.

## 3.3 Gardner, "Observations in the Course of Contracts"

1. Four principles underly ethical problems in contracts:[84]

    (a) *The Tort Idea*: promisor must pay for losses from promisee's reliance.

    (b) *The Bargain Idea*: buyer must pay the agreed price to the seller.

    (c) *The Promissory Idea*: promises are inherently binding.

    (d) *The Quasi-Contractual Idea*: anyone who receives anything of value should pay for it unless it's a gift.

2. The first and last principles suggest justice happens *after* the transaction, and courts exist to correct deals gone wrong.

3. In the second and third principles, parties settle justice *before* their voluntary transaction.

---

[83] Casebook p. 3.
[84] Casebook p. 4.

# § 4 Consideration

1. Consideration is giving something and getting something in return. Both parties get something they want from the other.

2. Consideration is the thing that locks up a contractual relationship—"[s]omething (such as an act, a forbearance, or a return promise) bargained for and received by a promisor from a promisee . . . "[85]

3. Why do we require consideration?

4. Can you sell a bottle of Gatorade for $10,000? Yes—courts are hesitant to interfere with private transactions (with a few exceptions).

5. Spectrum of ways a contract can be established:

    (a) **Objective**: forms, labels, seals, magic words.

    (b) **Subjective**: intent—e.g., the intent to make a promise.

6. Consideration traditionally has two elements:

    (a) Mutual assent.

    (b) Exchange of value.

7. "The rule that a mere verbal promise, without any consideration, cannot be enforced by action, is universal in its action, and cannot be departed from to suit particular cases in which a refusal to perform such a promise may be disgraceful."[86]

## 4.1 Donative Promises, Form, and Reliance

### 4.1.1 Donative Promises

Made for affective reasons, usually informal, and not demonstrably relied upon.[87]

#### 4.1.1.1 Gifts: *Dougherty v. Salt*

Donative promises are not enforceable.

1. A boy's aunt gave him a promissory note for $3,000, payable at her death or before. The aunt died. The boy's guardian brought an action against the aunt's estate to recover the promised money.

2. The jury found for the plaintiff. The trial judge set aside the verdict and dismissed the complaint. The appellate court reversed and reinstated because it held that the promissory note was valid consideration.

---

[85] Black's Law.
[86] Casebook p. 153.
[87] Casebook p. 6.

## 4 CONSIDERATION

3. The New York Court of Appeals (Cardozo) reversed, holding that the note was "the voluntary and unenforceable promise of an executory gift."[88] The note was inadequate consideration in this context because paper does not make a donative promise enforceable.

#### 4.1.1.2 Restatement Second § 1: Definition

1. "A contract is a promise or a set of promises for the breach of which the law gives a remedy, or the performance of which the law in some way recognizes as a duty."

#### 4.1.1.3 Restatement Second § 17: Requirement of a Bargain

1. " . . . a contract requires a bargain in which there is a manifestation of mutual assent to the exchange and a consideration."

2. But, there are many exceptions.

#### 4.1.1.4 Restatement Second § 71: Requirement of Exchange; Types of Exchange

- (1) Consideration must be bargained for.

- (2) A performance or return promise is "bargained for" if sought and given in exchange.

- (3) Performance can be an act, forbearance, or creation, modification, or destruction of a legal relation.

- (4) Performance may be given to another person.

#### 4.1.1.5 Restatement Second § 79: Adequacy of Consideration; Mutuality of Obligation

1. If the consideration requirement is met, there are no requirements of gain/loss, equivalence in value, or "mutuality of obligation."

#### 4.1.1.6 On the Restatement Second

1. Samuel Williston, Reporter for the Restatement First: contract law is "a set of axioms that were deemed to be self-evident, together with a set of subsidiary rules that were purportedly deduced from the axioms."[89]

2. Arthur Corbin, Consultant to the Restatement Second: father of "modern contract law."[90]

---

[88]Casebook p. 7.
[89]Casebook p. 8.
[90]Casebook p. 8.

### 4.1.1.7 Consideration

1. Acceptance alone is not consideration, but at some point acceptance becomes an act that qualifies as consideration.

    (a) The **Tramp Example**: I'll call the store and have two suits ready for you. You go to the store and find out I was just kidding. There's no act there. But what if I make you drive to a store in San Francisco? Is that an act that constitutes consideration? I got what I wanted (for you to go to the store) and you thought you were getting what you wanted (new clothes).

2. Courts generally do not consider the adequacy of consideration.

3. The **mutuality rule** required both parties to be obligated to each other, but it did not require equal consideration.

4. Two conceptions: broad and narrow.

5. *Broad*: "consideration" refers collectively to the things that make contracts legally enforceable—e.g., bargain or reliance.[91]

6. *Narrow*: "consideration" is the same thing as "bargain." The Restatement Second adopts this approach, known as the **bargain theory of consideration**.

7. The bargain theory of consideration creates two kinds of distortion:

    (a) *Terminological*: many other elements besides bargain can make a contract enforceable. Therefore, "under the terminology of the Restatement Second, a promise needs consideration to be enforceable unless it does not need consideration to be enforceable."[92]

    (b) *Substantive*: the bargain theory presumes that all nonbargain promises are unenforceable. It does not allow the law to develop other means of making promises enforceable.

### 4.1.1.8 Gifts

1. The common law distinguishes between gifts and promises to make gifts. A promise to make a gift is not enforceable. *Dougherty*.

2. A **deed of gift** (or **inter vivos document of transfer**) transfers ownership via a written instrument.[93]

3. Another way to make a gift is for the owner to declare herself a **trustee** of her property for the benefit of another. The trustee retains legal title but the beneficiary receives beneficial ownership.[94]

---

[91] Casebook p. 8.
[92] Casebook p. 9.
[93] Casebook pp. 9–10.
[94] Casebook p. 10.

## 4 CONSIDERATION

4. Once given, a gift cannot be taken back—but before it's given, we're uncertain.

### 4.1.1.9 Donative Promises

1. A donative promise is a promise to make a gift, without any expectation of getting anything in return.

2. Why make a donative promise, rather than wait and give the gift later?

    (a) Instincts vary. The promisor might think she has better judgment right now than she will in the future.

    (b) The promisor wants to derive satisfaction from the promisee's gratitude.

    (c) **Beneficial reliance**: the promisee can rely on the promise to her benefit—e.g., knowing that her Aunt will pay for college, a niece decides to finish high school, rather than look for a paying job.

3. The "basic fault line" in classical contract law was between bargain promises (enforceable) and gratuitous promises (unenforceable).

4. Should contract law be based on the moral belief that breaking promises is unethical, or should it promote utilitarian goals like "compensating injured promisees and increasing social wealth"?[95]

5. Lon Fuller introduced **substantive** and **process** bases for enforcing promises.

    (a) The two process bases are evidentiary (making sure a promise has actually been made) and cautionary (preventing inconsiderate action by the promisor).

    (b) Simple donative promises are problematic on both bases. They raise problems of proof (evidence may be uncertain) and deliberativeness (the promisor is likely to be emotionally involved with the promisee).

    (c) Substantive reasons for enforcing donative promises include compensating the promisee's disappointment (a form of injury), move assets from the wealthy to the less wealthy, and increase the likelihood of beneficial reliance. But these substantive bases are open to question.

### 4.1.1.10 Conditional Donative Promises

1. In a bargain promise, the condition is the **price** of the promise—e.g., I'll give you $20 if you mow my lawn.

2. In a conditional donative promise, the condition is the **means** to make the gift—e.g., I'll buy you a car if you pick one that costs less than $15,000.

3. We have to rely on a "reasonable interpretation" to determine whether a condition is a means or a price.[96]

---

[95]Casebook p. 11.
[96]Casebook p. 13.

## 4 CONSIDERATION

### 4.1.2 Form

1. We often look for an official indication of a valid agreement, like wax seals, but power of form has mostly evaporated.

#### 4.1.2.1 Von Mehren, "Civil-Law Analogues to Consideration: An Exercise in Comparative Analysis"

1. French, German, and common law systems recognize four policies that lead them to treat a transaction as unenforceable:

    (a) **Evidentiary**: Evidentiary security—protecting against manufactured evidence and dealing with insufficient proof.

    (b) **Cautionary**: Safeguarding the individual against his own rashness.

    (c) **Channeling**: Signaling to make sure that the promisor knows the promise is enforceable.

    (d) **Deterrent**: Unwillingness to enforce contracts of "suspect or marginal value."[97]

#### 4.1.2.2 Channeling Function of Contract-Law Rules

1. Von Mehren's channeling policy assumes actors know contract law—but must don't. So, this policy only applies to rules that actors are likely to know.

#### 4.1.2.3 No Enforcement without Consideration: *Schnell v. Nell*

Ritual is not enough. To be valid, consideration must impose a legal obligation.

1. Zacharias Schnell's wife Theresa agreed to pay $200 each to Nell and the two Lorenzes on her death. After she died, Schnell agreed with the three claimants to pay out the promised money over three years. In exchange, the three claimants gave him one cent. Schnell later decided he wanted to back out of the agreement.

2. Schnell argued that there was no consideration because his wife did not own any property and therefore could not make such a promise. The lower court sustained a demurrer against Schnell.

3. The question was whether the contract "express[ed] a consideration sufficient to give it legal obligation, as against Zacharias Schnell."[98]

4. The court considered three bases for consideration:

---

[97] Casebook pp. 13–14.
[98] Casebook p. 15.

## 4 CONSIDERATION

(a) First, the claimants promised to pay Schnell one cent. Although courts generally do not evaluaate the adequacy of consideration, this exchange—one cent for $200—is too unconscionable to sustain. ("Even in traditional times, courts were not willing agents of absurdity or oppression."—Berring.)

(b) Second, Mr. Schnell bore love and affection to his late wife, and "she had done her part, as his wife, in the acquisition of the property."[99]. This was invalid because these are past considerations and have no bearing on Schnell's promise to the three claimants.

(c) Third, Mrs. Schnell wished to give the money to the three claimants. This was invalid because she had no property of her own.

### 4.1.2.4 Form

1. Formal elements (wax seals, etc.) used to create special legal effect, but their use is waning.

2. One consequence of the removal of legal effect of formal devices is that there is no longer any device to make a donative promise binding. Some states have adopted statutes that make written instruments enforceable. European countries have implemented systems that weigh a range of factors involved in a donative promise, like the promisor's financial situation and the grantee's acts of ingratitude.[100]

### 4.1.3 Reliance and Promissory Estoppel

1. A moral obligation to keep a promise is generally insufficient to establish a legal obligation.

2. Lawmakers should also consider social policy and experiential concerns (e.g., problems of proof).

3. Injury from reliance is a moral and policy reason for enforcing promises.

### 4.1.3.1 No Reliance in Traditional Common Law: *Kirksey v. Kirksey*

These facts are analogous to the tramp example. Was this a mere gift or was there consideration? The defendant got nothing in return for his offer, but the plaintiff *did* do what he wanted—so you can start the consideration analysis.

1. "Dear Sister Antillico . . . "

---

[99]Casebook p. 15.
[100]Casebook pp. 22–23.

2. The defendant, plaintiff's brother in law, invited the plaintiff and her family to come live at his house, offering her living space and land to tend, but asking nothing in return. She abandoned her property in the country to come live with him. He let her live comfortably in the house for two years. Then, he put her in a house, "not comfortable," in the woods, and then made her leave.

3. The lower court found for the plaintiff for $200.

4. The judge writing the opinion for the Supreme Court of Alabama believed that the "loss and inconvenience" she suffered justified the award, but the majority believed the offer was a "mere gratuity." Reversed.[101]

### 4.1.3.2 Restatement Second § 90: Promise Reasonably Inducing Action or Forbearance

1. "A promise which the promisor should reasonably expect to induce action or forbearance on the part of the promisee or a third person and which does induce such action or forbearance is binding if injustice can be avoided only by enforcement of the promise. The remedy granted for breach may be limited as justice requires."

### 4.1.3.3 Estoppel in Pais and Promissory Estoppel

1. Under classical contract law, only a bargain was consideration. Donative promises were not enforceable, even if the promisee relied on the promise. *Kirksey*.[102]

2. *Ricketts*: a man promised his granddaughter $2,000 so she would not have to work anymore. She quit her job. The man died. The granddaughter successfully brought suit. The court avoided the question of whether reliance constituted consideration. Instead, reliance estopped the man's estate from pleading a lack of consideration. This case lies somewhere between estoppel in pais and promissory estoppel.

3. **Estoppel in pais** (or equitable estoppel): if A made a statement and B foreseeably relied on that statement, A is estopped from denying that statement's truth. Based on a *statement of fact*. For instance, say a store receives a suspicious check. It calls the owner of the bank account to make sure it's valid. The owner absent-mindedly said yes, but the check was in fact a forgery. The customer is estopped from denying the truth of his statement.[103]

4. **Promissory estoppel**: a promise is binding if the promisee reasonably relied on it. Codified in Restatement Second § 90. Based on a *promise*.

---

[101] Casebook pp. 24–25.
[102] Casebook p. 25.
[103] See Understanding Contracts p. 139.

## 4 CONSIDERATION

5. Both are instances of a broader **"reliance principle"**: "When one person, A, uses words or actions that he knows or should know would induce another, B, to reasonably believe that A is committed to take a certain course of action, and A knows or should know that B will incur costs if A doesn't take action, A should take steps to ensure that if he doesn't take the action, B will not suffer a loss."[104]

### 4.1.3.4 Promissory Estoppel Problem

1. An uncle promises his nephew $50,000 to buy a business. The nephew buys the business with his own money. The uncle dies before depositing the promised money. The executor of the uncle's estate refuses to recognize the nephew's claim.

2. Can the nephew base an action on:

   (a) Deceit? (No. The uncle did not try to conceal anything.)
   
   (b) Estoppel in pais? (No. The dispute does not turn on the truth of of a factual statement.)
   
   (c) A promise made enforceable by unbargained-for reliance? (Yes.)
   
   (d) A promise supported by a bargained-for consideration? (No. There was no bargain.)

### 4.1.3.5 Promissory Estoppel: *Feinberg v. Pfeiffer Co.*

Feinberg planned her retirement on the basis of the company's promise to pay her a pension. Her reliance made the promise binding.

1. Facts:

   (a) 1910: Feinberg began working for Pfeiffer.
   
   (b) 1947: Still working for Pfeiffer, now in more senior positions.
   
   (c) December 27, 1947: the company resolved to raise her salary to $400/month and offer a lifetime retirement pay of $200 per month (but with the hope that she would continue working).
   
   (d) June 30, 1949: Feinberg retired and began collecting her monthly payments.
   
   (e) Spring 1956: the company's new ownership refused to continue sending the monthly retirement checks.
   
   (f) April 1, 1956: the company sent its final check, for $100. Feinberg refused it and brought suit to recover her full monthly retirement checks.

2. The trial judge held for Feinberg and awarded $5,100.

---
[104]Casebook p. 27.

3. Pfeiffer raised two peripheral arguments on appeal:
    (a) The court erroneously allowed evidence that at the time of trial, Feinberg could not seek employment because she was suffering from cancer.
        i. Held: this was not the basis for the trial court's decision.
    (b) There was insufficient evidence to support the court's finding that (1) Feinberg would not have quit unless she relied on the monthly retirement checks and (2) Feinberg did in fact rely on the checks after retiring.
        i. Held: the lower court properly credited Feinberg's testimony that she relied on the checks.
4. The key issue was whether Feinberg had a right to recover her retirement checks on the basis of a contractual obligation.
    (a) Pfeiffer: the company's decision to give the retirement checks was a mere promise to make a gift. Donative promises are not enforceable unless supported by consideration. The only possible consideration here was a reward for past service, which is not valid. Further, Feinberg's position was at-will.
    (b) Feinberg: agreed that a promise based on past services would not constitute valid consideration, but (1) she continued to work for a year and a half after the company's resolution and (2) she based her decision to retire on reliance on the monthly check.
    (c) Court:
        i. Feinberg's first contention, that she continued to work after the resolution, does not constitute valid consideration because that was not a condition of the agreement.
        ii. But Feinberg's second argument, that she relied on the promise, was valid. The promise met the Restatement Second § 90 requirements for promissory estoppel (in fact, one of the Restatement illustrations involves retirement annuities).
        iii. Affirmed.

### 4.1.3.6 Distinguishing *Feinberg*: *Hayes v. Plantations Steel Co.*

An employee cannot claim reliance on a retirement pension if the employer's promise did not affect his decisionmaking.

1. Plantations Steel told Hayes it would "take care" of him upon his retirement, but there was no mention of an actual sum. It gave a first payment "as a token of appreciation" and implied that the payments would continue annually.

## 4 CONSIDERATION

2. The company changes ownership. Later owners discontinued the payments. Hayes brought suit.

3. The key distinction from *Feinberg* is that the company's offer of annuities was not an inducement to retire, because Hayes had given notice of retiring several months earlier. He did not rely on the company's promise because nothing about the promise changed his behavior. Therefore, the promise did not meet the requirements for promissory estoppel.

4. Would it matter if the check had come annually for 10 years? 30 years?

    (a) He chose to retire before the offer.

    (b) He expressed the uncertainty by showing up each year and wondering if the check was there for him.

### 4.1.3.7 Remedies and Consideration

1. To what extent should a promise be enforced?

2. For more, see the Remedies section below.

3. Two types of **injury**:[105]

    (a) **Reliance interest**: the promisee is worse off than he would have been if the promise had not been made. **Reliance damages** restore a promisee to the position he would have been in had the promise not been made.

    (b) **Expectation interest**: the promisee is worse off than he would have been if the promise had been performed. **Expectation damages** restore the promisee to the position he would have been in had the promise been performed.

4. Two types of **reliance damages**:

    (a) **Out-of-pocket costs**: costs incurred by promisee prior to the breach.

    (b) **Opportunity costs**: the surplus the promisee would have enjoyed if he had taken the opportunity that the promise led him to forgo.

5. To what extent should a relied-upon donative promise be enforced? Should it be the extent of the reliance (the **reliance measure**) or the full expectation of the promise (the **expectation measure**)? See casebook pp. 37–38.

6. The expectation measure can be useful where reliance damages are difficult to establish but obviously significant.[106]

---

[105] Casebook p. 35.
[106] Casebook p. 39.

## 4.1.3.8 Goldstick v. ICM Realty

1. The expectation measure is valuable because it's simple, and it often covers opportunity costs that the reliance measure misses.[107]

## 4.1.3.9 Reliance Damages vs. Expectation Damages: *D & G Stout, Inc. v. Bacardi Imports, Inc.*

D & G suffered significant damages from its reliance on Bacardi's promise. Bacardi was liable for reliance damages.

Lesson 1: get it in writing. Lesson 2: create consideration in the agreement, e.g., exchange money, in order to guarantee enforceability of the promise.

1. D & G, operating as General Liquors, faced the dilemma of whether to sell out or scale down. Bacardi promised it would continue to deal with General as its Northern Indiana distributor. Relying on this promise, General turned down the selling price it had been offered from National Wine & Spirits. A week later, Bacardi withdrew its account, forcing General to sell at a much lower price–$550,000 lower than National's original offer.

2. Can General recover the difference in price from Bacardi? Trial court: no. Bacardi's promise was not one on which it should reasonably expected General to rely.[108]

3. Indiana followed Restatement Second § 90 on promissory estoppel.

4. Appellate court:

    (a) In at-will employment relationships in Indiana, employees cannot sue for lost wages, but they *can* sue for moving expenses incurred on the basis of a promise.[109]

    (b) This is the distinction between reliance damages (moving expenses—*Eby*) and expectation damages (lost anticipated wages—*Ewing*).

    (c) Was General's loss the result of lost expectations of future profit (expectation damages) or an opportunity foregone in reliance on the promise (reliance damages)?

    (d) In its negotiations, General relied on Bacardi's promise. The devaluation of the company as a result of the broken promise was a reliance injury, analogous to moving expenses.

    (e) Reversed.

---
[107] Casebook p. 40.
[108] Casebook p. 42.
[109] Casebook p. 42.

### 4.1.3.10 Promissory Estoppel and Expectation Damages: *Walters v. Marathon Oil Co.*

The Walters reasonably relied on Marathon's promise to let them open a dealership. The court awarded remedies to put the Walters in the position they would have been in if the contract had been performed (expectation damages).

1. Mr. and Mrs. Walters hoped to open a gas station. Relying on promises from Marathon Oil, the Walters bought and renovated and abandoned service station. Before signing the final agreement, Marathon put a moratorium on new applications for dealerships. The Walters brought suit.

2. The Walters argued that they should be able to recover lost potential profits, totaling $22,200 (370,000 gallons at six cents per gallon).

3. Marathon argued that the Walters should only be able to recover for their reliance injury, i.e., the difference between their expenditures on the site (purchase and renovations) and its present value—and actually, real estate values increased, so they really made a small profit.

4. The trial court sided with the Walters and the appellate court agreed, holding that the Walters had forgone the opportunity to make their investment elsewhere.

5. "Since promissory estoppel is an equitable matter, the trial court has broad power in its choice of a remedy . . . "[110]

## 4.2 The Bargain Principle

1. Consideration exists when the promise is part of an exchange. Both parties receive something in exchange for their promise—a "bargained-for exchange."

2. The "two major props of the bargain principle" are **fairness** and **efficiency**.[111]

3. Moral obligations alone are generally insufficient to establish consideration.

4. Under classical contract law, one-sided contractual modifications, where only one party changes its obligations, are not enforceable because there has been no consideration.

### 4.2.1 The Bargain Principle

1. "It is an elementary principle, that the law will not enter into an inquiry as to the adequacy of consideration."[112] *Westlake v. Adams, C.P.*

---

[110]Casebook p. 45.
[111]Casebook p. 59. See also Eisenberg, "The Bargain Principle and Its Limits" below.
[112]Casebook p. 47.

#### 4.2.1.1 Benefit and Detriment: *Hamer v. Sidway*

"'Consideration' means not so much that one party is profiting as that the other abandons some legal right in the present, or limits his legal freedom of action in the future, as an inducement for the promise of the first."[113]

1. William E. Story, Sr. promised his nephew, William E. Story, 2d, $5,000 if he would avoid drinking, gambling, etc. until he was 21. When Story 2d reached 21, he and his uncle agreed that the uncle would keep the money until Story 2d was mature enough to manage it, at which point he would receive the $5,000 plus interest. Story Sr. died without transferring the money. Story 2d brought suit against the estate's executor to recover.

2. The executor argued that Story 2d, the promisee, was not harmed, but benefited, and that Story Sr., the promisor, was not benefited. He argued that "unless the promisor was benefited, the contract was without consideration."[114]

3. The court here disagreed, holding that consideration exists when "something is promised, done, forborne, or suffered by the party to whom the promise is made as consideration for the promise made to him."[115]

#### 4.2.1.2 Statute of Frauds

1. What promises must be in writing to be enforceable?

2. Lesson: get it in writing.

#### 4.2.1.3 Defining Detriment: *Davies v. Martel Laboratory Services, Inc.*

"Detriment" can include giving up freedom of action, even if it generally "benefits" a person. In this case, there was consideration because the company got what it wanted.

1. Davies was an at-will employee of Martel. Martel offered her a deal in which she would become a permanent vice president if she earned an MBA, and Martel offered to pay for half of the degree. Davies enrolled in an MBA program. Martel fired her a year later.

2. Martel argued that there was no consideration because the pursuit of an MBA was a benefit to Davies, not a disadvantage or detriment.

3. The trial court granted summary judgment for Martel.

4. The appellate court reversed, holding that Martel's definition of "detriment" was inaccurate. Legal detriment also means giving up the privilege to do something.

---

[113] Casebook p. 49.
[114] Casebook p. 49.
[115] Casebook p. 49.

### 4.2.1.4 Bad (or Great) Deals: *Hancock Bank & Trust Co. v. Shell Oil Co.*

Bad (or great) deals are binding.

1. Hancock bought land after making a deal with Shell that Shell would lease the land for fifteen years at very low rent, with the option to renew for another fifteen years or to terminate the lease with 90 days' notice.

2. The bank then tried to get out of the agreement, arguing that the 90 days' notice provision in a fifteen-year lease is "so lacking in mutuality as to be void against public policy."[116] The court disagreed, holding that if there is valid consideration, parties cannot escape a contract simply because they realized they got a bad deal.

### 4.2.1.5 Restatement Second § 71: Requirements of Exchange; Types of Exchange

1. Consideration exists only if the promise is bargained for.

2. Performance is bargained for if is sought and given.

3. Performance can consist of:

    (a) Act.

    (b) Forbearance.

    (c) Creation, modification, or destruction of a legal relation.

4. Performance may be given to the promisor or some other person.

### 4.2.1.6 Restatement Second § 72: Exchange of Promise for Performance

1. Any performance that is bargained for is consideration (except for cases in § 73, legal duty, and § 74, settlement of claims).

### 4.2.1.7 Restatement Second § 79: Adequacy of Consideration; Mutuality of Obligation

1. If there is consideration, there is no requirement of gain/detriment, equivalence in values exchanged, or mutuality of obligation.

---
[116] Casebook p. 51.

### 4.2.1.8 Selling Money: *Batsakis v. Demotsis*

It's possible to sell money. Loan agreements are enforceable even if the amount to be repaid is orders of magnitude larger than the amount loaned.

This case is distinct from *Schnell v. Nell* in two ways. First, the $25 in this case was not meant as a gift. It was a real exchange, which may have meant the difference between life and death under the circumstances.[117] Second, this case involved exchanging foreign currency. The act of exchanging currency in a market created consideration.

1. During World War II, Batsakis loaned the equivalent of $25 to Demotsis. Demotsis agreed to pay him $2,000 plus interest as soon as she could access her American accounts. Demotsis signed a letter indicating that she received $2,000 and would repay it with interest. Batsakis sued to recover the $2,000 plus interest.

2. The trial court awarded $750 plus interest, on the half-baked theory that half-restitution would be fair (—half-baked because contracts are binary: you either have a contract or not, and you can't just cut it in half).

3. Demotsis argued that the contract did not have valid consideration because she only received $25. The appellate court disagreed. Batsakis essentially sold $25 to Demotsis at the price of $2,000 plus interest. "Defendant got exactly what she contracted for according to her own testimony."[118] The court awarded $2,000 plus interest.

### 4.2.1.9 Sweet-Escott, Greece—A Political and Economic Survey, 1939–1953

1. Greece was in crisis during World War II. This was the context for *Batsakis*. Batsakis perhaps took advantage of Demotsis under the circumstances, weakening his argument that consideration was valid.

### 4.2.1.10 Consideration and Remedies

1. To what extent should a particular type of promise be enforced?

2. This problem doesn't matter when the three types of damages—expectation, reliance, and restitution—produce identical results. For instance, if a homeowner fails to pay a plumber $60 for an hour of work, the plumber's expectation damages were $60, and his reliance damages were also likely $60 because he could have been working for the same rate on another job.

3. But sometimes the damages differ. In *Batsakis*, for instance, the defendant argued that the value of what she received was far less than the value she promised. She was willing to repay the $25 she received (restitution damages) but not the value of what she had promised (expectation damages).

---

[117]See *Understanding Contracts* pp. 88–89.
[118]Casebook p. 54.

## 4 CONSIDERATION

4. In *Batsakis*, both parties agreed that the contract was enforceable, but they differed on the extent. So when the court said it would not review the adequacy of consideration, it was saying that the normal remedy for breach of contract is expectation damages, and it doesn't matter whether the value of one promised performance exceeded the value of the other.[119]

### 4.2.1.11 Restatement Second § 175: When Duress by Threat Makes a Contract Voidable

1. A contract is void when:

    (a) When the victim had no choice but to assent because of a threat.

    (b) When a third party creates duress, unless the other party to the transaction in good faith did not know of the duress and gives value or relies on the transaction.

### 4.2.1.12 Restatement Second § 176: When a Threat is Improper

1. A threat is improper when it is:

    (a) A crime or tort.

    (b) Criminal prosecution.

    (c) Bad faith civil process.

    (d) Breach of duty of good faith and fair dealing.

### 4.2.1.13 UNIDROIT Principles of International Commercial Contracts Art. 3.9: Threat

1. A threat invalidates a contract if the threat is "so imminent and serious as to leave the first party no reasonable alternative" but to agree

2. (The UNIDROIT Principles was an attempt to develop a framework for international contract law.)

### 4.2.1.14 Principles of European Contract Law § 4.108: Threats

1. A threat invalidates a contract if (1) the threat was wrongful in itself or (2) wrongful to use as a means to obtain the conclusion of the contract, unless the threatened party had a reasonable alternative.

---
[119]Casebook p. 55.

# 4 CONSIDERATION

### 4.2.1.15 Duress: *Chouinard v. Chouinard*

Driving a hard bargain is not wrongful.

1. The Chouinard family owned Arc Corporation. Fred ran the business. Al, his father, and Ed, Fred's twin brother, both claimed they each owned 37.5% of the company, or about $500,000 each.

2. After a bad financial decision, Fred managed to secure a loan commitment from the Heller Company. But Heller refused to make the loan until the ownership dispute was settled, so Fred's attorney drafted an instrument under which all parties would agree that Heller could make the loan but no one would acknowledge anyone else's ownership claim. Al and Ed's attorney rejected the proposal because they wanted to take the opportunity to settle the ownership fight. Fred agreed to pay Ed and Al $95,000 each, mostly in promissory notes, in exchange for their release of their claims to ownership of the company.

3. Fred then brought suit to set the promissory notes aside. He argued that the contract was void because it was made under duress resulting from "impending bankruptcy" and "financial peril." The court disagreed, holding that Ed and Al had driven a hard bargain but had not acted wrongfully. "We conclude, therefore, that there is simply no duress shown on this record, for one crucial element is missing: a wrongful act by the defendants to create and take advantage of an untenable situation. Ed and Al had nothing to do with the financial quagmire in which Fred found himself, and we cannot find duress simply because they refused to throw him a rope free of any 'strings.'"[120]

### 4.2.1.16 Rescue and Salvage: *Post v. Jones*

The rules against duress prevent a rescuer from unfairly profiting from the rescue. However, the rules of salvage create an incentive to rescue, striking a balance between the rescuer's effort and the victim's need.

1. The Richmond, a whaling ship, ran aground with a full hold of whale oil. Three other whaling ships sailed by. The captain of the Richmond agreed to auction off its oil to the other three ships. Upon return, the Richmond's owners brought suit to recover the value of the oil the other ships took, arguing that the other ships were entitled to "salvage" but not to the oil at the auction price.

2. The court held for the Richmond's owners, reasoning that the auction transactions were invalid because "one party had absolute power, and the other no choice but submission." The rules of salvage allow the rescuers to

---
[120] Casebook p. 57.

be compensated for their effort, but the court was not willing to "permit the performance of a public duty to be turned into a traffic or profit."[121]

### 4.2.1.17 Eisenberg, "The Bargain Principle and Its Limits"

1. *The Desperate Traveler*: T is stranded in the desert. G passes by and offers a ride for two-thirds of T's wealth or $100,000, whichever is more.

2. Under traditional contract doctrine, this agreement would be enforceable. The duress limitation applied only if the promisee was responsible for putting the promisor in a position of distress. But the passerby didn't cause the desperate traveler's distress.

3. But that outcome serves neither fairness nor efficiency.

4. The maritime salvage doctrine is a reasonable solution. It prevents the rescuer from exploiting the one in distress, but it includes a "generous bonus to provide a clear incentive for action and compensation for the benefit conferred."[122]

### 4.2.1.18 New York Gen. Bus. Law § 396-r: Price Gouging

1. Sellers cannot take "unfair advantage of consumers during abnormal disruptions of the market."[123]

### 4.2.1.19 Price Gouging: *People v. Two Wheel Corp.*

1. A power generator seller ran afoul of the New York price gouging rule.

## 4.2.2 Unconscionability

### 4.2.2.1 Lack of Meaningful Choice: *Williams v. Walker-Thomas Furniture Co.*

"Unconscionability has generally been recognized to include an absence of meaningful choice on the part of one of the parties together with contract terms which are unreasonably favorable to the other party."[124]

This contract probably still would have been unconscionable if the buyer had been a sophisticated lawyer, but it would have been a closer case.

1. Over five years, the plaintiffs bought furniture from Walker-Thomas on its installment plan, which provided that if the buyer defaulted on any item, Walker-Thomas could repossess every item purchased at the store. Plaintiffs argued that the contracts were unconscionable and thus unenforceable.

---

[121] Casebook p. 58.
[122] Casebook p. 60.
[123] Casebook p. 60.
[124] Casebook pp. 65–66.

2. The trial and appellate courts held for Walker-Thomas, finding "no ground upon which this court can declare the contracts in question contrary to public policy."[125]

3. The D.C. Circuit disagreed, holding that unconscionability includes "an absence of meaningful choice on the part of one of the parties together with contract terms which are unreasonably favorable to the other party."[126]

4. Remanded to determine whether the contracts were unconscionable.

5. Many states later passed statutes to outlaw this type of installment contract.

### 4.2.2.2 UCC § 2-302: Unconscionable Contract or Clause

1. Courts can strike or modify unconscionable contracts.

### 4.2.2.3 Uniform Consumer Credit Code § 5.108: Unconscionability

1. Courts can strike or modify unconscionable contracts.

2. Factors in determining unconscionability include:

    (a) Seller's knowledge that the buyer will not benefit.

    (b) Gross disparity between product/service and price.

    (c) Seller takes advantage of buyer's infirmities (illiteracy, etc.).

### 4.2.2.4 Federal Trade Commission Regulations—Door-to-Door Sales

1. A detailed enumeration of unfair door-to-door sales practices.

### 4.2.2.5 The Uniform Commercial Code

1. The UCC aims to unify commercial law among the states.

2. The UCC applies only to "goods."

3. Many states have adopted the UCC in whole or in part.[127]

---

[125] Casebook p. 65.
[126] Casebook pp. 65–65.
[127] Casebook pp. 72–74.

### 4.2.2.6 Applying the UCC: *Pittsley v. Houser*

1. The UCC applies only to "goods." This contract involved the purchase of a carpet (a good) and its installation (a service). The question was whether the UCC applied.

2. The "predominant factor" test asks whether the bulk of the contract involved goods or services.

3. Another approach allows the goods and services portions of the contract to be severed.

4. The court here applied the predominant factor test, holding it was advantageous to treat the contract as a whole, since the UCC aims to simplify and clarify contract law. It found that the UCC applied.

### 4.2.2.7 Comments to the UCC

1. In states that have adopted the UCC, the legal status of the accompanying comments is unclear.

### 4.2.2.8 UNIDROIT Principles of International Commercial Contracts Art. 3.10: Gross Disparity

1. Taking unfair advantage of the other party's circumstances or limitations can invalidate a contract.

### 4.2.2.9 Principles of European Contract Law §§ 4.109, 4.110

1. Largely the same as UNIDROIT § 3.10 above.

### 4.2.2.10 Commission of the European Communities, Council Directive 93/13/EEC

1. Detailed specifications about what constitutes an unfair contract.

### 4.2.2.11 Substantive and Procedural Unconscionability: *Maxwell v. Fidelity Fin. Servs., Inc.*

The court distinguished between **substantive unconscionability** (one-sidedness) and **procedural unconscionability** (fine-print surprises). It held that substantive unconscionability alone is sufficient to invalidate a contract.

1. December 1984: a door-to-door salesman sold the Maxwells a water heater for $6,512 on an installment plan. The unit was never installed properly and never worked properly. The total purchase price after all installments was $15,000. As part of the deal, the financing company, Fidelity, placed a lean on the Maxwell house.

2. 1988: Elizabeth Maxwell wanted to borrow $800 from Fidelity for an unrelated issue. Fidelity drew up a new contract that included the outstanding water heater balance, the $800 loan, and a life insurance policy.

3. Maxwell made payments until 1990, at which point she asserted that the contract was unconscionable and therefore unenforceable.

4. Fidelity argued that the 1988 contract "worked a novation," barring any action on the 1984 contract. The trial court granted summary judgment for Fidelity and the appellate court affirmed.

5. The court here distinguished between substantive unconscionability ("an unjust or one-sided contract") and procedural unconscionability (fine print surprises, etc.).[128] It held that substantive unconscionability alone was sufficient to invalidate a contract, and that there was sufficient evidence to raise a question of "grossly-excessive price."[129] Reversed.

### 4.2.2.12 Classical and Modern Contract Law

1. Contract law reasoning:

    (a) *Substantive legal reasoning*: validity of a doctrine turns on normative considerations (morals, policy, etc.).

    (b) *Formal legal reasoning*: law consists of doctrines that are autonomous from policy, morality, and experience.

    (c) *Axiomatic legal reasoning*: "fundamental doctrines can be established on the ground that they are self-evident."[130]

    (d) *Deductive legal reasoning*: most doctrines follow from syllogisms beginning with more fundamental doctrines.

    (e) Classical contract law coupled axiomatic and deductive reasoning.

    (f) By contrast, modern contract law reasoning justifies doctrines on the basis of morality, policy, and experience.

2. Contract law can be plotted along four axes:

    (a) Objectivity (directly observable state of the world) $\leftrightarrow$ subjectivity (mental state).

    (b) Standardization (depends on abstract variables) $\leftrightarrow$ individualization (depends on situation-specific variables).

    (c) Static (depends on what occurred at the moment the contract was formed) $\leftrightarrow$ dynamic (depends on moving streams of events before and after the contract).

---

[128] Casebook p. 79.
[129] Casebook p. 81.
[130] Casebook p. 83.

# 4 CONSIDERATION

(d) Binary (e.g., no damages or expectation damages) ↔ multifaceted (e.g., no damages, expectation damages, reliance damages, restitution damages).

3. Many other limits on contracts are surrogates for unconscionability.[131]

## 4.2.3 Mutuality

1. "As a contract defense, the mutuality doctrine has become a faltering rampart to which a litigant retreats at his own peril."[132] *Helle v. Landmark, Inc.*

### 4.2.3.1 Corbin, "The Effect of Options on Consideration

1. B must actually agree to limit his behavior as A requests for the contract to be binding. Otherwise, it's an illusory contract.

### 4.2.3.2 Williston on Contracts § 103B

1. Illusory promises are not consideration.

### 4.2.3.3 Restatement Second § 77: Illusory and Alternative Promises

1. A promise is not consideration if the promisor reserves alternatives, unless the alternatives would have been consideration or would have been eliminated.

### 4.2.3.4 Illusory Promises

1. There is no consideration without commitment.

2. A valid promise shrinks the promisor's freedom of choice. An illusory promise does not shrink freedom of choice. Since there is no commitment, there is no consideration.

3. Example: A offers to deliver up to 5,000 bushels of wheat at $2/bushel to B within 30 days. B has not promised to buy any wheat.

4. Another example: A offers to buy 100 pounds of potatoes a month from B, but only if A is in the mood for potatoes that month. A has not made a commitment, so the promise is not enforceable.

5. **The illusory promise rule has mostly disappeared.**[133] The illusory promise rule is an implication of the mutuality requirement. If one party can freely abandon the agreement, there is no mutuality and therefore no

---
[131] Casebook p. 86.
[132] Casebook p. 100.
[133] Casebook p. 98.

consideration. Today, courts only find a lack of mutuality if one party has *complete* discretion to abandon the contract, which is rare. In addition, we require parties to perform in good faith. So, the illusory promise rule has been confined to a very narrow range of scenarios.

### 4.2.3.5 Unequal Terms: *Lindner v. Mid-Continent Petroleum Corp.*

As long as there has been sufficient consideration, unequal terms do not invalidate a contract.

1. Linder leased a filling station to Mid-Continent for three years. Mid-Continent retained the right to terminate the lease at any time with ten days' notice. Lindner tried to cancel the lease on the ground that it lacked mutuality. The court upheld the contract on the ground that ten days' minimum rent constituted consideration, and that the unequal terms of the contract did not invalidate the agreement.

### 4.2.3.6 Reluctant Seller, Eager Buyer: *Gurfein v. Werbelovsky*

1. A contract for the order for glass plates allowed the buyer to cancel at any time. The buyer repeatedly requested performance. The seller tried to get out of the contract, arguing that it was void because the buyer's promise was illusory. The court held that there was consideration because the seller could have bound the buyer by immediately shipping the order when it was placed.

### 4.2.3.7 Satisfaction Clauses: *Mattei v. Hopper*

Satisfaction clauses constitute consideration when courts read them as requiring good faith. Otherwise, the satisfaction clause would not involve a commitment, so the promise would be illusory.

1. The plaintiff, a real estate developer, offered $57,000 to buy the defendant's land. The defendant accepted. The developer included a clause in the contract that stipulated that the agreement was subject to "obtaining leases satisfactory to the purchaser." It wanted to make sure it could find a tenant before it bought the land.

2. The defendant then tried to back out of the deal. The plaintiff indicated it had obtained leases and offered to pay the balance of the full purchase price. Defendant declined. The plaintiff developer sued for damages, and the defendant landowner argued that the plaintiff's promise was illusory. The court held for the plaintiff. Such "satisfaction" clauses are valid because the promisor's "duty to exercise his judgment in good faith is an adequate consideration to support the contract . . . "[134]

---
[134] Casebook p. 100.

### 4.2.3.8 No Equivalence Required for Consideration: *Harris v. Time, Inc.*

Any bargained-for act or forbearance constitutes consideration. There is no mutuality requirement.

1. The plaintiff received a letter from Time magazine offering a free calculator watch if he opened the envelope. He did, and discovered he could get the watch only if he also subscribed to Fortune magazine. He brought a class action suit against Time, alleging that the envelope's promise was a binding agreement. The court agreed, holding "*any* bargained-for act or forbearance will constitute adequate consideration for a unilateral contract . . . Courts will not require equivalence in the values exchanged or otherwise question the adequacy of the consideration."[135]

2. However, the court dismissed the action on the basis of *de minimis non curat lex*.

### 4.2.3.9 "Primitive Stage of Formalism": *Wood v. Lucy, Lady Duff-Gordon*

The intent of the parties outweighs "primitive formalism."

1. Lady Duff-Gordon gave the plaintiff the exclusive to sell her endorsements to put on others' designs. He brought suit because she put her endorsement on other products without his knowledge and withheld profits.

2. Lady Duff-Gordon argued that the contract was invalid because it did not bind the plaintiff to anything.

3. Cardozo: "The law has outgrown is primitive stage of formalism when the precise word was the sovereign talisman and every slip was fatal."[136] The clear intent of the parties was to give the plaintiff an exclusive right. The defendant cannot escape that right on a formal technicality.

### 4.2.3.10 UCC § 2-306: Output, Requirements, and Exclusive Dealings

1. Terms dealing with expected output, requirements, and exclusive dealings must be followed in good faith.

### 4.2.3.11 Requirements and Output Contracts

1. *Requirements contract*: a seller agrees to provide as much of a good as the buyer requires.

---

[135] Casebook p. 101.
[136] Casebook p. 102.

2. *Output contract*: a buyer agrees to buy all of a seller's output.

3. Traditionally, "courts often refused to enforce requirements contracts where the buyer could choose to have no requirements."[137] But both parties shrunk their realm of choice, so there was mutual consideration.

4. UCC § 2-306 requires good faith in requirements contracts.

5. " . . . a modern court would almost certainly hold that all requirements and output contracts have consideration."

### 4.2.4 Legal Duty, Modification, and Waiver

1. Promises to perform an act that the promisor was already obligated to do are unenforceable.[138]

2. Most companies say they wouldn't enforce strict compliance if the other party requested modification of the contract.[139]

3. Initial contracts require consideration, but changes to existing agreements do not. *Watkins & Son v. Carrig*.[140]

#### 4.2.4.1 No Enforcement for Legal Duty: *Slattery v. Wells Fargo Armored Serv. Corp.* "The performance of an existing duty does not amount to the consideration necessary to support a contract."[141]

1. Wells Fargo offered a $25,000 reward for information on a robbery and shooting. A polygraph operator discovered the perpetrator while questioning him on an unrelated matter. The court denied him the reward because he "was under a pre-existing duty to furnish his employers with all useful information revealed to him through interrogation of the perpetrator.

#### 4.2.4.2 *Shadwell v. Shadwell*

1. Affirming the unenforceability of legal duty as consideration.

#### 4.2.4.3 Restatement Second § 73: Performance of Legal Duty

1. Performance of a legal duty is not consideration.

#### 4.2.4.4 N.Y. Penal Law §§ 200.30, 200.35

1. It is illegal to give gratuities for a public servant, and for a public servant to take them

---

[137]Casebook p. 103.
[138]Casebook p. 107.
[139]Casebook pp. 126–27.
[140]Casebook pp. 141–42.
[141]Casebook p. 108.

### 4.2.4.5 Thin Line Between Legal Duty and No Duty: *Denney v. Reppert*

A sheriff's deputy out of his jurisdiction was not under a legal duty to make an arrest.

1. A bank association offered a reward for the apprehension of a bank robber. Several bank employees and state policemen were ineligible because they were performing their legal duty in apprehending the criminal. However, a sheriff's deputy could get the reward because he made the arrest while out of his jurisdiction.

### 4.2.4.6 Extortion is not Consideration: *Lingenfelder v. Wainwright Brewery Co.*

1. Lingenfelder was the executor of the estate of Jungenfeld, who had contracted as an architect for the Wainwright Brewery Co. When Jungenfeld learned that Wainwright had awarded the refrigeration contract to another company, Jungenfeld called off his work. The brewery agreed to pay him five percent of the cost of the competitor's refrigeration machine if Jungenfeld would complete his contracted work.

2. Wainwright argued that Jungenfeld's actions amounted to extortion. The court held that Jungenfeld was already under a legal obligation to finish the job. Performing his legal duty did not constitute consideration.

### 4.2.4.7 Extortion and Legal Duty: *Austin Instrument, Inc. v. Loral Corp.*

The legal duty rule did not prevent Austin from extorting higher prices from Loral, but the court held for Loral under the theory of duress.

1. Loral contracted to provide radar equipment to the Navy. Loral subcontracted with Austin to provide components. Before an order had been filled, Austin stopped work and demanded a price increase. Austin consented, but wrote a letter saying it did so only under duress.

2. The New York Supreme Court, appellate division, held that Austin's price increases were in good faith and did not constitute duress.

3. The New York Court of Appeals reversed, holding that this was a "classic case" of duress.[142] The possibility of defaulting on its Navy contract posed a serious threat to Loral.

---
[142] Casebook p. 121.

### 4.2.4.8 More on the Legal Duty Rule

1. The legal duty rule is based on a *static* view of contract, because the terms of a contract are entirely fixed when parties make the agreement.

2. A regime under which modifications are enforceable reflects a *dynamic* view of contract, in which contracts are constantly evolving processes.

### 4.2.4.9 Substitute Contracts: *Schwartzreich v. Bauman-Basch, Inc.*

If parties mutually agree to a new contract, the new contract is enforceable and the old contract is voided.

1. The plaintiff contracted to work for the defendant at $90/week. He got another offer for $100/week. He and the defendant agreed to sign a new contract for $100/week. The defendant argued that the new contract was void, but the court held that as long as the parties mutually agreed to enter into the new contract, it was enforceable.

### 4.2.4.10 Restatement First § 406, Illustration 1

1. In a bilateral contract, if "each party surrenders something he might have retained," there is consideration for the substitute contract.

### 4.2.4.11 UCC §§ 3-103(a)(4), 3-104, 3-311

1. 3-103(a)(4): definition of good faith.

2. 3-104: definition of a negotiable instrument.

3. 3-311: satisfaction of claims by instrument.

### 4.2.4.12 Restatement Second § 279: Substituted Contract

1. The substituted contract replaces the original contract.

### 4.2.4.13 Restatement Second § 281: Accord and Satisfaction

1. *Accord*: "a contract under which an obligee promises to accept a stated performance in satisfaction of the obligor's existing duty."

### 4.2.4.14 The Legal Effect of the "Executory Accord"

1. *Accord*: an agreement under which a new obligation replaces an existing obligation.

2. *Executory accord*: an unperformed accord.

3. *Satisfaction*: performance of the accord.

4. Historically, the executory accord was unenforceable—"one of the major mysteries of the common law."[143] The common law rule was "inconsistent with the bargain principle, basically inexplicable, and wrong."[144]

5. **Substituted contract**: the earlier agreement is immediately discharged.

6. Courts are likely to find that an accord is a substituted contract if the original duty "was disputed, unliquidated, had not matured, and involved a performance other than the payment of money."[145] For instance, for agricultural services, A agreed to pay B in cattle. They disagreed over how many cattle were due. They agreed that A would pay three sheep instead. Courts will likely treat the accord as a substituted contract.

7. Courts are likely to find that an accord is *not* a substituted contract if the original duty "was undisputed, liquidated, had matured, and involved the payment of money."[146] For instance, A agreed to pay $900 for B's services, and A does not dispute B's claim. They agree that A will give two sheep instead of paying $900. Courts will likely *not* find that the accord is a substituted contract.

8. Other rules:

    (a) *Performance*: if an accord involving a different performance is executed, the original contractual obligations are discharged.

    (b) *Suspension of old contract*: "an executory accord operates to suspend A's rights under the original contract during the period in which B is supposed to perform the accord."[147]

    (c) If one party fails to perform under the accord, the other party can sue under either the new accord or the old contract.

9. "... in many or most jurisdictions the traditional rule concerning accord and satisfaction has been substantially or almost completely eroded."[148]

## 4.2.4.15 Restatement Second § 89: Modification of Executory Contract

1. A promise modifying an earlier contract is binding when:

    (a) It's fair;

    (b) Provided by statute; or

    (c) "justice requires enforcement" if a party relies on it.

---

[143] Casebook p. 135.
[144] Casebook p. 136.
[145] Casebook pp. 136–37.
[146] Casebook p. 137.
[147] Casebook p. 137.
[148] Casebook p. 138.

### 4.2.4.16 No Consideration for Modification: *Angel v. Murray*

Modifications do not require consideration as long as the parties agree voluntarily.

1. Maher had a series of five-year contracts with the city for garbage collection. In 1967, he requested an additional $10,000 because the city's population had grown unexpectedly fast. The council agreed. They also granted an extra $10,000 for the following year.

2. Angel, a Newport resident, brought suit to recover the extra $20,000.

3. The trial court found that Maher was not entitled to the extra $20,000 because the contract required him to collect all refuse within the city, regardless of population increases—i.e., Maher had a preexisting duty to collect all of the city's garbage.

4. "It is generally held that a modification of a contract is itself a contract, which is unenforceable unless supported by consideration."[149]

5. "The modern trend appears to be to recognize the necessity that courts should enforce agreements modifying contracts when unexpected or unanticipated difficulties arise during the court of the performance of a contract, even though there is no consideration for the modification, as long as the parties agree voluntarily."[150]

6. In this case, since the modification was fair and voluntary, the agreement was enforceable. Reversed.

### 4.2.4.17 UCC § 2-209: Modification, Rescission, and Waiver

1. Modifications do not require consideration.

### 4.2.4.18 CISG Art. 29

1. CISG governs the sale of international goods.[151]

2. Art. 29: modification requires only agreement. Exchange is not required.

### 4.2.4.19 Waiver: *Clark v. West*

Clauses are waivable.

---

[149]Casebook p. 139.
[150]Casebook p. 140.
[151]UN Convention on Contracts for the International Sale of Goods. See supplement p. 358.

## 4 CONSIDERATION

1. Plaintiff contracted to write law books to be published by defendant (West). The contract included a clause that gave the plaintiff $4 per page, but only $2 per page if he did not abstain from "intoxicating liquors."[152] Plaintiff did not abstain but otherwise delivered on the contract.

2. Plaintiff argued that West knew about his drinking but did nothing about it, which amounted to a waiver of that part of the contract.

3. The court held that the abstinence clause was not consideration for the contract. Rather, it was a condition precedent. "It is not a contract to write books in order that the plaintiff shall keep sober, but a contract maintaining a stipulation that he shall keep sober so that he may write satisfactory books."[153]

4. The court held that the clause was waivable as a matter of law. It remanded it to the lower court to determine whether it was in fact waived.

### 4.2.4.20 Restatement Second § 84: Promise to Perform a Duty in Spite of Non-Occurrence of a Condition

1. A party can waive conditions of a contract. For instance, A hires B to build a house. As part of the agreement, A will only pay after A's architect, C, has signed off. C refuses to approve because of trivial defects. A tells B he'll pay him anyway. A has waived the condition and his promise is binding.

### 4.2.4.21 *Nassau Trust Co. v. Montrose Concrete Prods. Corp.*

1. Modification requires consideration, and is therefore binding. Waiver does not require consideration, so it is not binding until executed.

2. Can this be reconciled with *Angel v. Murray*, above?

### 4.2.4.22 Waiver under the UCC: *BMC Indus., Inc. v. Barth Indus., Inc.*

1. "[T]he UCC does not require consideration or detrimental reliance for waiver of a contract term."[154]

## 4.3 Past Consideration

### 4.3.1 Restatement Second § 82: Promise to Pay Indebtedness; Effect on the Statute of Limitations

1. A promise to pay earlier contractual indebtedness is binding, even if the earlier debt would have been barred by the statute of limitations.

---

[152] Casebook p. 144.
[153] Casebook p. 146.
[154] Casebook p. 149.

### 4.3.2 Restatement Second § 83: Promise to Pay Indebtedness Discharged in Bankruptcy

1. If a debt was discharged during bankruptcy, a later promise to pay it is binding.

### 4.3.3 Three Situations in Which a Promise to Discharge an Unenforceable Obligation is Binding

1. Traditionally, there were three cases when a promise to pay based on a past event, rather than a present bargain, were enforceable:[155]

    (a) A promise to pay a debt barred by the statute of limitations.

    (b) A promise by an adult to pay a debt incurred when the person was underage.

    (c) A promise to pay a debt that has been discharged in bankruptcy.

2. Explanations:

    (a) Infants and debtors have moral obligations to pay their debts. When they recognize this moral obligation by making a promise, the promise becomes binding.

    (b) The creditor actually had a legal claim, but the debtor had a valid defense (infancy or bankruptcy). When the debtor makes a promise to pay the debt, he waives his defense.

        i. Why not require consideration for the promise to pay the debt?

### 4.3.4 No Past Consideration: *Mills v. Wyman*

Moral obligations do not make promises enforceable. Past consideration is required.

1. Levy Wyman fell ill in Hartford on return from a voyage from sea. The plaintiff, Daniel Mills, housed him at his expense for 15 days, at which point Wyman died. Wyman's father promised to pay Mills's expenses.

2. When Wyman's father failed to pay, Mills sued. The trial court directed a nonsuit.

3. There was no consideration in the defendant's promise to pay Mills. Moral obligation is insufficient without consideraion. " . . . if there was nothing paid or promised for it, the law, perhaps wisely, leaves the execution of it to the conscience of him who makes it. It is only when the party making the promise gains something, or he to whom it is made loses something, that the law gives the promise validity."[156]

---

[155] Casebook p. 151.
[156] Casebook p. 154.

## 4 CONSIDERATION

### 4.3.5 Protection as Consideration: *Webb v. McGowin*

Protecting McGowin from injury was sufficient consideration for McGowin's later promise to pay Webb to be binding.

1. Webb worked in a lumber company. He was pushing heavy wooden blocks off a ledge. As he was pushing a block, he noticed that McGowin was below. The only way he could prevent the block from crushing McGowin was to fall with it, so he did, and sustained serious injuries and suffered permanent disabilities.

2. McGowin promised to pay Webb $15 every two weeks for the rest of Webb's life, until McGowin died a few years later. McGowin's executors refused to keep paying. Webb brought suit.

3. "Where the promisee cares for, improves, and preserves the property of the promisor, though done without his request, it is sufficient consideration for the promisor's subsequent agreement to pay for the service, because of the material benefit received."[157]

4. McGowin's promise was therefore enforceable.

### 4.3.6 Saving from Decapitation: *Harrington v. Taylor*

Voluntary humanitarian acts are not consideration.

1. The defendant assaulted his wife and she took refuge in the plaintiff's house. The defendant came to the plaintiff's house. She tried to decapitate him with an axe. The plaintiff caught it, saving the defendant's life but badly mutilating her hand. The defendant agreed to pay for the plaintiff's damages, but failed to pay.

2. The court held that "a humanitarian action of this kind, voluntarily performed, is not such consideration as would entitle her to recover at law."[158]

### 4.3.7 Restatement Second § 86: Promise for Benefit Received

1. Promises for previous benefits are "binding to the extent necessary to prevent injustice." But promises are not binding if they are gifts or if th value of the promise is disproportionate to the benefit.

### 4.3.8 ALI 42d Annual Proceedings

1. Past consideration is *sometimes* binding. Some cases are "gratuitous transactions" (with no consideration) and "quasi-contracts" (with consideration, if justice requires).[159]

2. The ALI seems to be struggling here to pin down a rule.

---
[157] Casebook p. 157.
[158] Casebook p. 160.
[159] Casebook p. 160–61.

### 4.3.9 Note on Past Consideration

1. If A confers a benefit on B without B's prior request, the subsequent relationship could fall into three categories:

    (a) B is legally obligated to compensate A under the law of *unjust enrichment*—for instance, if A paid B money by mistake.

    (b) B is morally but not legally obligated to compensate A—for instance, if B has suffered a loss on rescuing A. *Mills v. Wyman.*

    (c) B is neither morally nor legally obligated to compensate A—e.g., ordinary gifts.

2. At common law, the general rule was that promises based on past benefits were unenforceable.

3. The Restatement Second makes promises based on past benefits enforceable on the basis of unjust enrichment. Fuller and Eisenberg argue that they should instead be enforceable on the basis of moral obligation.[160]

## 4.4 The Limits of Contract

1. When are contracts inappropriate?

### 4.4.1 *Balfour v. Balfour*

1. Agreements do not always create legally binding contracts—for instance, two people agreeing to go on a walk. The parties did not intend that legal consequences would attend the agreement.

### 4.4.2 In Vitro Fertilization: *In Re the Marriage of Witten*

How much judicial interference do we want in marital relations? How does public policy determine when contracts should be enforced?

The court here held that In vitro fertilization agreements are enforceable, but either party can change his or her mind up to the point of the use or destruction of the embryo.

Courts are generally hesitant to impose "coercive parenting"—i.e., forcing someone to have a child.

1. Trip and Tamera wanted a divorce. They had frozen fertilized embryos. Tamera wanted to use the embryos to have a child. Trip objected.

2. Before starting the in vitro fertilization process, Trip and Tamera signed an "Embryo Storage Agreement" stipulating that any use or transfer of the embryos required both of their consent. The one exception allowed unilateral action if the other died. There was no provision for divorce.

---
[160] Casebook p. 162.

## 4 CONSIDERATION

3. Tamera raised three arguments for custody of the embryos: (1) the storage agreement is silent on the possibility of divorce, (2) it would be in the child's best interests, and (3) it would violate public policy to allow Trip to back out of the agreement.

4. *Best interests*: no. There was no child to care for.

5. *Scope of storage agreement*: the agreement did not specifically account for divorce, but release of the embryo nonetheless required both parties' consent. The question was whether the agreement was enforceable. The court tested three approaches:

   (a) *Contractual approach*: contracts entered into at the time of in vitro fertilization are enforceable if they are not contrary to public policy. On the one hand, agreements would have little force if they were not enforceable. On the other hand, parents may not know their true feelings until the child is born.

   (b) *Contemporaneous mutual consent*: both partners should have an equal say in how the embryo is used.

   (c) *Balancing test*: agreements are enforceable, but either party can change his or her mind up to the point of use or destruction of any stored embryos. In case of disagreement, the court must evaluate both parties' interests. But should courts be the decision makers in these kinds of situations?

6. "We think . . . it would be against the public policy of this state to enforce a prior agreement between the parties in this highly personal area of reproductive choice when one of the parties has changed his or her mind concerning the disposition or use of the embryos."[161]

7. Held: the agreements are enforceable, but any party can change his or her mind up to the point of the use or destruction of the embryos. If the parties cannot agree, the status quo remains (for up to 10 years).

### 4.4.3 Who is a Parent?

1. Domestic partners are responsible for child support.

### 4.4.4 Surrogacy Agreements: *R.R. v. M.H.*

Surrogacy agreements (in Massachusetts) are unenforceable if they involve money or if they require the mother to give up the child before four days after birth.

1. A man paid a woman $10,000 to be the surrogate mother of his child.

---
[161] Casebook p. 170.

2. "Policies underlying our adoption legislation suggest that a surrogate parenting agreement should be given no effect if the mother's agreement was obtained prior to a reasonable time after the child's birth or if her agreement was induced by the payment of money."[162] An agreement that violates these policies is unenforceable.

3. "A surrogacy agreement judicially approved before conception may be a better procedure . . . "[163]

### 4.4.5 Surrogate-Parenting Legislation

1. Seventeen states have surrogacy legislation. The statutes vary widely.

### 4.4.6 42 U.S. Code § 274e: Prohibition of Organ Purchases

1. Human organs cannot be transferred for "valuable consideration."[164]

### 4.4.7 Radin, "Market-Inalienability"

1. Radin is responding to Posner's argument that any bureaucratic solution will be flawed, so we should allow organs to be sold on the open market.

2. "In precluding sales but not gifts, market-inalienability places some things outside the marketplace but not outside the realm of social intercourse."[165] Some things shouldn't be commodified—children, organs, sexual services, and so on.

---

[162] Casebook p. 183.
[163] Casebook p. 185.
[164] Casebook p. 185.
[165] Casebook p. 186.

# § 5 Remedies

## 5.1 Introduction to Contract Damages

### 5.1.1 Restatement Second § 344: Purposes of Remedies

1. **Expectation**: puts promisee in the position he would have been in if the contract had been *performed*. You get what you bargained for.

2. **Reliance**: puts promisee in the position he would have been in if the contract had *not been made*.

3. **Restitution**: restores to the promisee any benefit he conferred to the promisor.

### 5.1.2 Expectation Damages: *Hawkins v. McGee*

The appropriate measure of damages is the difference between (1) performance of the contract as promised and (2) actual performance. In this case, damages are equal to the difference between the promised "perfect hand" and the actual state of the hand after the operation.

1. The plaintiff, Hawkins, had scar tissue on his hand that resulted from a severe burn from contact with an electrical wire. Dr. McGee removed the scar tissue and grafted some skin from Hawkins's chest onto his hand. Hawkins ended up in the hospital for three months and lost the use of his hand. Also, the new tissue apparently "filled his hand with a 'matted' and 'unsightly growth'—presumably hair."[166]

2. Hawkins sued for breach of an alleged warranty of the success of the operation. The trial court found for Hawkins. Hawkins also brought a negligence claim, which the trial court dismissed on nonsuit.

3. After trial, the defendant moved to set aside the verdict as excessive. The trial court ordered the verdict set aside unless Hawkins would remit all damages above $500. He refused. Exceptions on both sides were transferred to the Supreme Court.

4. Part 1: was there a contract, and if so, what were its terms?

    (a) The parties agreed that McGee had said that after the operation, Hawkins would be in the hospital for three or four days, and after going home, he would have a "perfect hand" for three or four days.[167] The court held that this alone would not have established a contract guaranteeing that Hawkins would *definitely* be home after three or four days or could go to work a few days after being home. It was

---
[166]Casebook p. 194.
[167]Casebook p. 190.

only an indication of the probable outcome of the surgery. But such a contract would have been established if Dr. McGee has promised a "*hundred per cent* perfect hand."

(b) But the question of the wording of the promise was irrelevant because Dr. McGee had "repeatedly solicited" the opportunity to perform the operation. He "sought an opportunity to 'experiment on skin grafting.'" Because these words constituted an inducement of consent, it was reasonable to conclude that the parties had entered into a contract.

5. Part 2: what damages were appropriate?

(a) The jury instructions requested damages for (1) pain and suffering and (2) "ill effects of the operation on the plaintiff's hand."[168]

(b) The appropriate damages would have been the difference between (1) the promised "perfect hand" and (2) the state of the hand after the operation. Pain and suffering were part of the bargain, and physical harm to the plaintiffs hand would be subsumed into the rule of damages the court adopted here.

6. Part 3: were McGee's requested jury instructions appropriate?

(a) No. They were "loosely drawn" and "extremely misleading."[169]

## 5.1.3 Cooter & Eisenberg, "Damages for Breach of Contract"

"The purpose of the social institution of bargain is to create joint value through exchange."[170] Protecting the expectation interest maximizes the value of contracts.

1. (A response to Posner's theory of efficient breach.)

2. Should we prefer reliance or expectation damages?

3. Sometimes, the difference doesn't matter. For instance, in a perfectly competitive market, reliance damages will equal expectation damages because the contract price will equal the forgone price the promisee could have contracted with a third party. But it matters if market conditions are far from perfectly competitive.

4. Traditionally, courts were united in the view that expectation damages were appropriate. "In fact, prior to the 1930's the reliance principle operated only in a covert manner."[171]

---

[168] Casebook p. 191.
[169] Casebook p. 193.
[170] Casebook p. 203.
[171] Casebook p. 200.

## 5  REMEDIES

5. The reliance principle expanded after § 90 of the Restatement Second (1932) and Fuller and Perdue, *The Reliance Interest in Contract Damages* (1934).

6. Should the reliance principle expand contract liability or reduce it by substituting reliance liability for expectation liability?

    (a) Reliance liability introduced a tort conception of liability.

    (b) There is not a clear rationale for expectation damages.

7. So: what should happen when reliance and expectation damages diverge?

    (a) *Efficiency*: the value created by a contract.

    (b) *Distribution*: how a contract's value is divided among the parties.

    (c) *Nonprice* terms of a contract make it possible to control a contract's efficiency.[172]

    (d) *Price* terms make it possible to control distribution.

    (e) Damages should be fair and efficient. " ... we take as a theorem that a damage rule is both fair and efficient if it corresponds to the terms that rational parties situated like the contracting parties would have reached when bargaining under ideal conditions."[173]

    (f) Would rational parties prefer reliance or expectation damages?

    i. *Administrative effects*: reliance is difficult to measure and prove, while expectation damages are based on the known contract price, rather than the speculative forgone price.

    ii. *Incentive effects*: if performance or alternative performance become more profitable than performance of the original contract, the promisor has to decide whether or not to breach. If there are only reliance damages, he will rationally breach. But if there are expectation damages, he will have to account for the promisee's loss of his share of the value of the contract. In other words, he will not internalize the value of the performance to the promisee.[174]

    iii. "Thus expectation damages create efficient incentives for the promisor's performance, while reliance damages do not, unless they are identical to expectation damages."

    iv. Expectation damages also give the promisee more confidence in planning.

---

[172]Casebook p. 201.
[173]Casebook p. 202.
[174]Casebook p. 202–03.

### 5.1.4 Actual Losses and Punitive Damages: *U.S. Naval Inst. v. Charter Commc'ns, Inc.*

Damages compensate parties for actual losses. Contract law does not recognize punitive damages.

1. Facts:
   (a) Plaintiff: US Naval Institute. Defendants: Charter Communications and Berkley Publishing Group.
   (b) September 1984: Naval (assignee of the copyright interests in *The Hunt for Red October*) agreed to grant Berkley exclusive paperback rights, not to be published before October 1985.
   (c) September 15, 1985: retail sales of the paperback began after Berkley shipped the books early.

2. The trial court dismissed, holding that Berkley was entitled as a matter of industry custom to ship the books early. The Second Circuit reversed, holding that the October 1985 start date must be upheld. After the initial remand, the trial court awarded Naval $35,380.50 in damages, $7,760.12 in profits wrongly received by Berkley, $15,319.27 in prejudgment interest on damages, and costs. Both parties appealed.

3. Berkley's pre-October sales were $724,300. Under copyright infringement, Naval sought all of the profits, as well as interest and costs.

4. Berkley argued that it could not be held liable for copyright infringement because it became the exclusive licensee of the paperback edition copyright on September 14, 1984, so Naval should not have been entitled to any recovery. At most, Naval had a contract claim, but Naval had disavowed that claim.

5. The trial court held that there was copyright infringement, and that Naval was entitled to "actual damages" and "profits 'attributable to the infringement.'"[175] It calculated the damages as its lost hardcover sales attributable to the paperback publication, i.e., the hardcover sales difference between August and September 1985, which amounted to $35,280.50. It calculate the lost profits as those from sales to customers who would not have bought the hardcover, or $7,760.12.[176]

6. On appeal (for the second time):
   (a) There was no copyright infringement because Berkley became the copyright holder on September 14, 1984. However, Naval was entitled to contract damages:
      i. " . . . the purpose of damages for breach of contract is to compensate the injured party for the loss caused by the breach."[177]

---
[175] Casebook p. 205.
[176] Casebook p. 205.
[177] Casebook p. 206.

Damages must therefore match the plaintiff's actual loss.
  ii. *Lost profits damages*: affirmed.
  iii. *Profits attributable to infringement*: plaintiff would not have received this income if the infringement had not occurred. The only purpose of these damages would be punitive, and contract law does not recognize punitive damages. Reversed.

### 5.1.5 Profiting from Breach: *Coppola Enters., Inc. v. Alfone*

"A seller will not be permitted to profit from his breach of contract with a buyer, even absent proof of fraud or bad faith, when the breach is followed by a sale of the land to a subsequent purchaser."[178]

1. Helen Alfone contracted with Coppola to buy a lot and home for $105,690. She put down a $10,568 deposit.

2. Coppola sent a letter informing Alfone of the tentative closing date. The closing date was to happen within 10 days of written notice.

3. Alfone tried but failed to find financing. Her lawyer requested an extension to pay the balance due on the property. Coppola refused and resold the property for $170,000.

4. The trial court found for Alfone, holding that Coppola had failed to act in good faith by allowing a reasonable time to close and by terminating the contract. She was awarded "benefit of bargain" damages for $64,310—i.e., the difference between Coppola's sale price to Alfone and the second seller—plus interest. Affirmed on appeal.

5. *Gassner v. Lockett*: an old and forgetful seller sold property to a buyer and then inadvertently sold it again to a second buyer at a higher price. Even though the seller acted in good faith, the first buyer was entitled to recover the seller's profits from the second sale.

6. Under the *Gassner* rule, Alfone was entitled to recover Coppola's profits.

### 5.1.6 Diminution in Value: *Laurin v. DeCarolis Constr. Co.*

1. The Laurins bought a home under construction from DeCarolis. While construction continued, DeCarolis bulldozed trees and removed gravel and loam. After paying the purchase price, the Laurins sued to recover the value of the lumber, gravel, and loam.

2. The trial court held that the Laurins were entitled to recover. The court here reversed, holding that the Laurins had contract rights rather than property rights—however, although the Laurins had not suffered a loss, DeCarolis was nonetheless liable because it "should not be allowed to retain is gains from a willful breach of contract."[179]

---

[178]Casebook p. 208.
[179]Casebook p. 209.

### 5.1.7 The Theory of Efficient Breach

1. Posner, theory of efficient breach: "breach of contract is efficient, and therefore desirable, if the promisor's gain from breach, after payment of expectation damages, will exceed promisee's loss from breach."[180]

2. **Resale paradigm**: A agrees to sell 100,000 widgets to B at $1 a piece. After A delivers 10,000 widgets, C says he desperately needs 25,000 widgets, and he's willing to pay $2 a piece. A agrees to sell to C. He makes a $1,250 profit on C's order, but it delays B's order, causing B $1,000 in damages. But even after paying expectation damages to B, A's breach still earned a profit of $250.[181]

3. Fuller and Eisenberg challenge the theory in the context of the Overbidder Paradigm, in which a seller breaches a contract with a buyer in favor of a sale with another buyer willing to pay more. They contend that efficient breach is inefficient in this case for three reasons:[182]

    (a) It remakes the parties' contract into a contract that allows and encourages sellers to seek overbidders.

    (b) It would reduce rewards for planning and investment.

    (c) It undermines the morality of promise keeping.

### 5.1.8 Rejecting Efficient Breach: *Greer Props., Inc. v. LaSalle Nat'l Bank*

Efficient breach is a breach of the covenant of good faith and fair dealing.

1. LaSalle agreed to sell land to Searle for $1.1 million, with Searle having the right to terminate the agreement if the soil was contaminated. The deal fell through because Searle discovered the soil was contaminated and would cost $500,000 to clean up.

2. LaSalle then contracted with Greer to sell the property for $1.25 million, with the option to terminate if the cost of cleanup became impracticable. It estimated the cost to be $100,000-$200,000.

3. LaSalle then negotiated a $1,455,000 contract with Searle and terminated its contract with Greer under the cleanup provision.

4. Greer brought suit for specific performance and damages. The trial court held for LaSalle. On appeal, the Seventh Circuit reversed, holding that by contracting with Greer, LaSalle had given up the right to seek a better price. Breaching the contract violated the covenant of good faith and fair dealing.

---

[180] Casebook p. 209.
[181] Casebook p. 210.
[182] Casebook pp. 210–14.

## 5.2 The Expectation Measure

### 5.2.1 Damages for Breach of a Contract to Perform Services

#### 5.2.1.1 Cost of Completion: *Louise Caroline Nursing Home, Inc. v. Dix Construction Co.*

If a contractor leaves a job unfinished, the client can recover cost of completion damages.

1. Dix breached a contract to build a nursing home.

2. An auditor found that Dix had breached the contract, but that Louise Caroline had suffered no compensable damages because "the cost to complete the nursing home was within the contract price less what had been paid to Dix"[183]—i.e., if the cost to completion was within the contract price, the nursing home could just pay another contractor to finish the job.

3. The nursing home argued that it was entitled to the difference between what Dix did and what it promised—i.e., expectation damages. It argued that it was entitled to the "benefits of its bargain."[184]

4. The court held that the principle underlying damages is that compensation "is the value of the performance of the contract." Applying this principle to the case of uncompleted construction contracts, the court held that damages "can only be in the amount of the reasonable cost of completing the contract and repairing the defendant's defective performance less such part of the contract price as has not been paid."[185] It affirmed the auditor's application of the "cost of completion" standard.

#### 5.2.1.2 Formulas

1. **Builder's damages for the owner's breach**:

    (a) The amount the owner owes the builder = (builder's expenditures incurred prior to the breach) + (lost profits) - (amount the owner paid prior to breach).

    (b) Example: A hires B to build a $500,000 house. B spent $400,000 on labor and materials, but the owner only paid $200,000 before breaching. B had no lost profits.

    i. A owes B expenditures ($400,000) + lost profits ($0) - amount paid prior to the breach ($200,000), or **$200,000**.

2. **Owner's damages for builder's breach**:

---
[183] Casebook p. 218.
[184] Casebook p. 218.
[185] Casebook p. 219.

(a) The amount the builder owes the owner = (total cost of completion) - (total original contract price - amount the owner already paid builder).

(b) Example: A hires B to build a $500,000 house. A pays the full $500,000 up front. B stops halfway through. B did $200,000 worth of work. It will cost $300,000 to finish the job.

   i. B owes A the cost of completion ($300,000) - ($500,000 - $500,000) = **$300,000**.

(c) Example: A hires B to build a $500,000 house. A hasnt paid anything. B stops halfway through. B did $200,000 worth of work. It will cost $300,000 to finish the job.

   i. B owes A the cost of completion ($300,000) - (original contract price ($500,000) - amount already paid ($0)) = -$200,000—i.e., A owes B $200,000.

### 5.2.1.3 Diminution in Value: *Peevyhouse v. Garland Coal & Mining Co.*

1. Garland contracted to strip mine on the Peevyhouse's farm. Garland agreed to perform remedial work on the land when it was done.

2. It turned out that the remedial work would cost $25,000 or more, but would result in only $300 in improvements to the property. Garland refused to perform.

3. The trial court directed a verdict in favor of the plaintiffs. It left the amount of damages to the jury, which returned an award of $5,000—less than the cost of performance but more than the value of the improvement to the land, and indeed more than the land itself.

4. The court held that in coal mining cases where remedial provisions are incidental, damages for breach of the remedial provision are limited to the diminution to the value of the property resulting from non-performance—in this case, $300.

5. Dissent: the parties were well aware of all the conditions when they signed the contract. The majority's holding "completely rescinds and holds for naught the solemnity of the contract before us and makes an entirely new contract for the parties."[186]

### 5.2.1.4 Affirming the *Peevyhouse* Rule: *Schneberger v. Apache Corp.*

The court affirmed the *Peevyhouse* "diminution in value" rule.

---

[186] Casebook p. 225.

1. Facts similar to *Peevyhouse* arose in Oklahoma. Apache Corp. drilled for oil on the Schnebergers' property. Restoration of the land would have cost $1.3 million, but the increase in property value would have been only $5,175.

2. The court affirmed *Peevyhouse*, despite recent statutory revisions. "... where the cost is grossly disproportionate to the cost of reclamation as in *Peevyhouse*, a review of recent case law suggests that courts are adhering to the diminution in value award . . ."[187]

### 5.2.1.5 Grossly Disproportionate: *H.P. Droher & Sons v. Toushin*

1. A homebuilder built a $44,000 house. A steel post was too low, causing the floor to sag significantly. It would have cost more than $20,000 to fix, but the benefit to the property value would have been far less than $20,000. The court held that the diminution in value rule (*Peevyhouse*) applies when "the cost of remedying the defects is grossly proportionate to the benefits . . ."[188]

### 5.2.1.6 Waste: *Eastern Steamship Lines, Inc. v. United States*

1. The government chartered a private vessel during WWII, promising to return it in the same condition. After the war, the owner sued the government for $4 million, which was the cost to return it to its prewar condition. But the value of the ship would have been only $2 million.

2. The court held that paying the full cost of restoration would be "a useless and wasteful expenditure of public funds . . ."[189]

### 5.2.1.7 Aesthetics and Good Faith: *City School Dist. of the City of Elmira v. McLane Const. Co.*

When the damages are aesthetically important, and when the builder does not act in good faith, the diminution in value rule does not apply. Rather, the owner can recover the full cost of repair.

1. A school district contracted for the construction of a swimming pool with special wooden beams. Repairs would have cost $357,000 for an increase in value of only $3,000. Because "the building was to be a showplace," and because the builder knew its methods would cause damage, the court held for the school district.

---

[187] Casebook pp. 230–31.
[188] Casebook p. 231.
[189] Casebook p. 232.

### 5.2.1.8 Residential vs. Commercial Construction: *Fox v. Webb*

1. " . . . a distinction exists between a contract to construct a dwelling for the owner who plans to live therein and a contract to construct a commercial structure where the aesthetic taste of the owner is not so deeply involved."[190]

### 5.2.1.9 Measuring Diminished Value: *Grossman Holdings Ltd. v. Hourihan*

Diminished value damages should be measured at the date of the breach, not the original date of the contract.

1. The contractor built the house backwards. The trial court held for the owner, but refused to award damages because (1) cost-of-completion damages would be wasteful and (2) diminished-value damages would be improper because the house's value had increased substantially since the date of the contract.

2. The appellate court held that diminished-value damages should be measured at the date of the breach.

### 5.2.1.10 Factfinder's Discretion: *Advanced, Inc. v. Wilks*

1. Cost-of-completion damages will sometimes put the owner in a better economic position than he would have been in if the contract had been fully performed. The factfinder should determine whether the owner is likely to pocket the difference or actually put it towards repairs.

### 5.2.1.11 "Pleasure and Amenity" Damages: *Ruxley Electronics & Construction Ltd. v. Forsyth*

1. Forsyth contracted with Ruxley to build a swimming pool with a maximum depth of 7'6." It ended up building a pool only 6' deep. The trial court found that 6' was safe for diving, so it did not award the cost of repair, £21,560. However, it did award "pleasure and amenity" damages of £2,500.[191]

2. Cost-of-completion and diminished-value damages are not the only possibilities. The measure should be "the loss truly suffered by the promisee."[192]

---

[190] Casebook p. 233.
[191] Casebook p. 235.
[192] Casebook p. 236.

## 5 REMEDIES

### 5.2.1.12 Calculating Damages: *Aiello Const., Inc. v. Nationwide Tractor Trailer Training and Placement Corp.*

1. Defendant agreed to pay $33,000 for construction work. It stopped paying after paying $10,500.

2. The trial court calculated damages for the plaintiff as as: plaintiff's costs so far ($21,500) plus expected profit from performance ($3,000) minus payments already made ($10,500) = $14,000, plus interest = $16,800.

### 5.2.1.13 *Formulas for Measuring Damages for Breach by a Person Who has Contracted to Have Services Performed*

1. There are two formulae for calculating a contractor's damages from the owner's breach:

    (a) Contractor's expenses + contractor's lost profits - amount paid by owner prior to breach. *Aiello*.

    (b) Contract price - cost of completion that the contractor saved - amount paid by owner prior to breach. Restatement Second § 346.

2. The two are algebraically equivalent, but courts usually use the second.

### 5.2.1.14 Restatement Second § 347: Measure of Damages in General

1. A contracts to build a house for B for $100,000. B breaches halfway through. A would have to spend $60,000 to finish. A's damages are the contract price ($100,000) - cost of completion that the contractor saved ($60,000) = $40,000. A can recover $40,000 minus any payments already made.[193]

### 5.2.1.15 Multiple Contracts: *Wired Music, Inc. v. Clark*

1. Wired provided music through rented telephone lines. Clark stopped paying, but another tenant at the same location offered to take up Clark's contract. Wired refused, and charged the new tenant a higher monthly rate. Wired sued to recover lost profits from Clark, minus the cost of renting the wire. The court held for Wired because it was possible for Wired to fulfill multiple contracts.

### 5.2.1.16 Overhead: *Vitex Mfg. Corp. v. Caribtex Corp.*

1. " . . . overhead should be considered to be a compensable item of damage."[194]

---

[193] Casebook p. 239.
[194] Casebook p. 241.

### 5.2.2 Damages for Breach of a Contract for the Sale of Goods: *Seller's* Breach

1. The UCC governs breach of contract for sale of goods. There are two types of buyer's remedies for a seller's breach:

   (a) Specific relief.
   (b) Damages.
      i. Remedies when the seller fails to deliver or the buyer rightfully revokes acceptance.
      ii. Remedies when the goods are defective (usually, breach of warranty).

#### 5.2.2.1 Cost of Repair Exceeds Purchase Price: *Continental Sand & Gravel, Inc. v. K & K Sand & Gravel, Inc.*

1. K & K sold Continental $50,000 worth of equipment with warranties. Continental sued for breach of warranty.

2. The trial court awarded $104,206.75 in damages.

3. K & K argued that Continental should only be able to recover from the diminution in value from the purchase price—i.e., the difference between the fair market value as accepted ($50,000) and the fair market value in defective condition. Under that formula, Continental could not recover more than $50,000.

4. Instead, the trial court applied UCC 2-714(2), which awards the difference between the value of the goods as accepted and the value of the goods if they had been as warranted. It held that the cost of repair was the proper standard.[195]

5. It's fine that the damages for breach of warranty (i.e., repair costs) exceed the value of the original machinery, because the reason the buyer made the deal in the first place was because the value of the goods to the buyer exceeded the purchase price.

#### 5.2.2.2 Direct Damages for Breach of Warranty: *Manouchehri v. Heim*

1. UCC § 2-714(2) sets the measure of direct damages for breach of warranty as the difference between the value of the goods as warranted and the value of the goods as accepted. Cost of repair is often a good approximation of this value, so courts commonly award it as direct damages.

---

[195] Casebook pp. 242–43.

## 5 REMEDIES

### 5.2.2.3 Cover: *Egerer v. CSR West, LLC*

1. 1995: Egerer needed fill to develop his land. He needed 17,000 more cubic yards than his normal supplier could supply (at $1.10 per cubic yard). CSR was engaged in an excavation project and agreed to sell all of its excavations to Egerer for $0.50 per cubic yard.

2. 1997: After delivering for two nights, changed circumstances made it more profitable for CSR to leave the material at the original site, so it stopped delivering to Egerer.

3. 1998: Egerer found a new supplier who quoted $8.25 per cubic yard.

4. 1999: Egerer found a new supplier and bought material at $6.39 per cubic yard.

5. 2000: Egerer sued CSR, alleging breach and demanding damages under the UCC.

6. There are two UCC remedies available to buyers when sellers fail to deliver goods sold:

    (a) *Cover*: the buyer purchases a replacement. Damages are the difference between the replacement price and the contract price. § 7-212.

    (b) *Hypothetical cover*: the buyer recovers the difference between the market price at the time of the breach and the contract price. § 7-213.

7. The trial court found that Egerer could recover under 7-213 for $8.25 per cubic yard, or $129,812.50 total.

8. On appeal, CSR agreed that 7-213 applied, but argued that $8.25 was not "the price for goods of the same kind," because the material was a different type.[196] It argued that the appropriate price was $1.10—the price from Egerer's original supplier.

9. The court held that $8.25 per cubic yard was appropriate because (1) the UCC allows courts to use goods of a different quality and (2) there was no evidence that suitable material was available at the time at a lower price.

### 5.2.2.4 *Panhandle Agri-Service, Inc. v. Becker*

1. Under the UCC, buyers can choose between cover and damages for non-delivery.

---
[196] Casebook p. 245.

### 5.2.2.5 J. White & R. Summers, "Uniform Commercial Code"

1. When a buyer has covered, can he ignore 2-712 and sue for a larger contract-market differential under 2-713?

2. The goal of contract remedies is to put the buyer in the position he would have been in if there had been no breach. But allowing a buyer to ignore 2-712 lets him wait to cover when market prices drop, and then recover under 2-713 for the higher damages of the earlier contract-market differential.

3. We should force covering buyers to use 2-712.

### 5.2.2.6 The Availability of Market-Price Damages to a Buyer Who Has Covered

1. The NCCSL and ALI updated the UCC to force covering buyers to use 2-712—but most states have not yet adopted the amendment.[197]

### 5.2.2.7 Incidental Damages: *Delchi Carrier SpA v. Rotorex Corp.*

Buyers can recover reasonable incidental damages related to the goods in question.

1. Facts:

   (a) January 1988: Rotorex agreed to sell 10,800 compressors to Delchi for its air conditioners to be delivered in three shipments before May 15. Rotorex sent a sample compressor that met Delchi's specifications.

   (b) March 26, 1988: Rotorex sent its first shipment, which arrived at Delchi on April 20.

   (c) May 9: Rotorex send a second shipment. While it was en route, Delchi discovered that the compressors were defective.

   (d) May 13: a Rotorex rep visited the Delchi factory. Delchi informed Rotorex that 93% of the compressors were unsuitable. Delchi asked Rotorex to supply new compressors. Rotorex refused.

   (e) May 23: Delchi canceled the contract. It expedited a previous order of compressors from Sanyo, but was unable to obtain substitutes from other sources, so it lost suffered sales losses during the 1988 season.

2. Delchi brought suit under CISG. In 1991, the court granted Delchi's motion for partial summary judgment. After discovery and a bench trial, the court found Rotorex liable for $1.2 million for (i) lost profits, (ii) expenses, (iii) expediting the Sanyo shipment, and (iv) handling and storing the rejected compressors.

---
[197] Casebook p. 247.

## 5 REMEDIES

3. The court denied Delchi's other claims—(i) shipping, etc., of the Rotorex compressors, (ii) obsolete parts to be used only for the Rotorex compressors, (iii) obsolete tooling, and (iv) labor costs when Delchi's factory was idle—on the ground that they were accounted for in its lost profits damages.[198]

4. Two arguments on appeal:

    (a) Rotorex: it did not breach the agreement and the calculation of damages was inappropriate.

    (b) Delchi: it was entitled to the expenses and lost profits that the trial judge denied.

5. Held:

    (a) *Breach*: Rotorex breached its contract.

    (b) *Damages award*: CISG awards damages for breach equal to the loss, including lost profits, not to exceed the amount which the party in breach foresaw (or should have foreseen). The trial court's damage award was appropriate. Moreover, Delchi should have won the expenses that the trial court denied. These expenses were legitimate and reasonably foreseeable.

    (c) On a few other issues of fact, the appellate court deferred to the trial court.[199]

### 5.2.3 Damages for Breach of a Contract for the Sale of Goods: *Buyer's* Breach

#### 5.2.3.1 *KGM Harvesting Co. v. Fresh Network*

When a buyer covers in good faith without reasonable delay, he can recover from the seller the difference between the cost of cover and the contract price. Whether the buyer can pass on the cost of cover to future buyers is irrelevant.

1. Facts:

    (a) July 1989: KGM and Fresh entered into a lettuce contract.

    (b) May 1991: the terms of the contract were settled. KGM would sell 14 loads per week to Fresh at $0.09/pound, or $55,440 per week.

    (c) May/June 1991: the price of lettuce increased dramatically. KGM refused to sell to Fresh at the contract price. Instead, it sold to others at a profit of $800,000 and $1.1 million.

---

[198]Casebook p. 249.
[199]Casebook p. 252–53.

5   REMEDIES                                                                 100

2. The issue was whether Fresh was entitled to damages from KGM for the cost of obtaining substitute lettuce. The jury awarded damages of $655,960.22, or the difference between the contract price and the cost of substitute lettuce during May and June. Subtracting the $233,000 Fresh owed KGM, Fresh won $422,960.22 and interest.

3. Fresh proceeded under UCC § 2-712: after the breach, it covered, and recovered the difference between the cover price and the contract price.

4. On appeal, KGM argued that Fresh should not be able to recover under § 2-712 because it was able to pass on its costs to subsequent buyers. Fresh suffered no actual loss, so damages would be a windfall.

5. *Allied Canners*: the buyer, Allied Canners, contracted to buy raisins from Victor, which it planned to resell to two Japanese companies at cost plus 4 percent. That year, the cost of raisins soared. Victor breached. Allied sued under the 7-212 formula, under which he would have won $150,000. The Japanese companies made no claim (one let it go and the other's claim expired under the statute of limitations). The court held that 7-212 damages should be limited to **actual loss** when three conditions apply:

    (a) The seller knew the buyer had a resale contract.

    (b) The buyer can't show it would be liable for damages on the forward contract.

    (c) The seller did not act in bad faith.

6. The court here held that the *Allied Canners* focus on good faith is inappropriate in commercial contexts. "[C]ourts should not differentiate between good and bad motives for breaching a contract in assessing the measure of the nonbreaching party's damages."[200]

7. Held: when a buyer covers in good faith without reasonable delay, he can recover from the seller the difference between the cost of cover and the contract price.

### 5.2.3.2   Recovery for Lost Profits under the UCC: *Neri v. Retail Marine Corp.*

1. Facts:

    (a) Neri contracted with Retail Marine to buy a boat for $12,587.40. He made a $40 deposit, increased shortly after to $4,250.

    (b) Six days later, Neri's lawyer sent a letter to Retail Marine rescinding his offer to buy the boat. But Retail Marine had already ordered the boat from the supplier, so it did not return Neri's deposit. Neri sued to recover his deposit.

---
[200] Casebook p. 259.

## 5 REMEDIES

(c) Retail Marine counterclaimed for breach of contract, also alleging damages of $4,250.

(d) Four months later, Retail Marine sold the boat to another buyer for the same price. Neri argued that Retail recouped its loss, while Retail argued that it could have sold two boats, earning two profits instead of one.

2. The trial court held that UCC 2-718(2) granted damages to put the seller in as good a position as performance would have done. It found that Retail had not suffered lost profits, so it awarded $500 to Retail and returned the remainder of the deposit ($3,750) to Neri.[201] Affirmed on appeal. (The $500 figure comes from UCC 2-718(2), which allows the buyer in breach can recover his payment minus 20% of performance or $500, whichever is smaller.)

3. The appellate court here noted that the buyer's recovery under UCC 2-718(2) is subject to offset if the seller can establish damages under another other UCC provisions. Here, Retail Marine was able to establish lost profits under 2-708 and incidental expenses under 2-710. Therefore, Neri should recover his deposit ($4,250) minus an offset for Retail Marine's lost profits ($2,579) and incidental expenses ($674), or $997.

### 5.2.3.3 Teradyne, Inc. v. Teledyne Industries, Inc.

1. A **lost volume seller** has the capacity to meet every potential sales order.

2. Read literally, the last clause of 2-708(2)—"due credit for payments or proceeds of resale"—prevents a seller from recovering from a buyer in breach if the seller can sell the item to another buyer for the same price.

3. However, in transactions with lost volume sellers, the buyer should not be credited with proceeds from the second sale, because the lost volume seller would have been able to make two profits instead of one.[202] Cf. Neri.

### 5.2.3.4 Childres and Burgess, "Seller's Remedies: The Primacy of UCC 2-708(2)"

1. "... the overwhelming proportion of sales contracts should products the 2-708(2) situation if repudiated by the buyer."[203]

### 5.2.3.5 R.E. Davis Chemical Corp. v. Diasonics, Inc.

1. What is the proper definition of "lost volume seller"? Courts often assume that a lost volume seller is one with "the capacity to supply the breached

---
[201] Casebook p. 261.
[202] Casebook p. 264.
[203] Casebook p. 264.

units in addition to what it actually sold."[204] But courts should also focus on whether it would be profitable for the seller to produce both units. At some point, it no longer becomes profitable for the lost volume seller to produce additional units. Thus, in some cases, awarding lost profits to lost volume sellers will result in overcompensation.

#### 5.2.3.6 Lost Profits for Second-Hand Cars: *Lazenby Garages Ltd. v. Wright*

Second-hand car dealers are not lost volume sellers because each used car is unique. If a buyer of a used car breaches, the seller cannot recover if it sells the same car to another buyer for the same price.

1. Facts:

    (a) February 19, 1974: Wright signed a contract with Lazenby to buy a BMW for £1,670.

    (b) February 20, 1974: Wright reneged.

    (c) April 23, 1974: Lazenby resold the car for £1,770 (or £100 more than Wright would have paid).

2. Lazenby claimed that it had bought the car for £1,325 and that Wright's breach cost them £345 in lost profits. Wright argued that they had lost nothing because they sold the car to another buyer. Lazenby argued that they sold many similar models, so Wright's breach cost them a sale.

3. The appellate court held that a dealer with several identical new cars might be able to prove lost profits. But since each used car is unique, used car dealers cannot claim lost profits if they sold the car in question to another buyer.

### 5.2.4 Mitigation; Contracts for Employment

#### 5.2.4.1 Duty to Mitigate: *Rockingham County v. Luten Bridge Co.*

1. Facts:

    (a) January 7, 1924: Rockingham County voted to award a bridge contract to Luten.

    (b) February 21, 1924: after some shuffling on the county board of commissioners, the county adopted a resolution declaring the bridge contract illegal and invalid. By this point, only about $1,900 worth of work had been done on the bridge. Luten continued construction despite the notice from the county.

---
[204]Casebook p. 265.

# 5  REMEDIES 103

   (c) March 3, 1924: the county passed a resolution to notify Luten than any further work on the bridge was at its own risk.

2. Luten sued to recover payment for the bridge.

3. The trial court held for Luten.

4. The question on appeal was whether Luten could recover for damages it incurred after receiving notice of breach from the county.

5. The court here found that Luten had a duty to mitigate damages once it received notice of the breach.

### 5.2.4.2  Duty to Mitigate for Modified Products: *Madsen v. Murray & Sons, Co.*

1. Seller manufactured pool tables. Buyer ordered 100 tables with special notches for electrical wiring. Buyer then breached. Rather than sell the customized tables, seller salvaged the parts it could and used the rest for firewood.

2. Seller sued for breach. It argued that it couldn't sell the modified tables because it would have harmed its reputation. The court held that the seller should have tried to sell them at market price or at least at a discount.

### 5.2.4.3  Reasonable Mitigation: *In Re Kellet Aircraft Corp.*

1. The defaulting party cannot dictate how the other party must mitigate. As long as the mitigating party acted reasonably, he has fulfilled his duty to mitigate.

### 5.2.4.4  "Slight Expense and Reasonable Effort" in Mitigating: *Bank One, Texas N.A. v. Taylor*

1. MBank wrongfully froze Taylor's assets, preventing her from participating in an oil drilling venture. MBank argued that Taylor could have used other personal assets to cover the costs of the venture. The court held that Taylor was not required to "make unreasonable outlays of money" or "sacrifice a substantial right of [her] own." She was required to make "only slight expense and reasonable effort."[205]

### 5.2.4.5  Defendant's Mitigation: *S.J. Groves & Sons Co. v. Warner Co.*

Where the defendant had an equal opportunity to mitigate loss, he cannot reasonably contend that the plaintiff failed to mitigate.

---
[205] Casebook p. 270.

## 5 REMEDIES

1. Groves won a subcontract on a Pennsylvania bridge project. It contracted with Warner for delivery of ready-mixed concrete.

2. Groves sued Warner, claiming losses resulting from Warner's failure to deliver.

3. The trial court held that at a certain date, Groves no longer had a reasonable expectation that Warner's performance would improve. It denied damages on the ground that Grove should have mitigated by hiring Trap Rock as a supplemental supplier.

4. The court here reversed, holding that Warner had an equal opportunity to mitigate damages by hiring Trap Rock itself.

### 5.2.4.6 Employees' Duty to Mitigate: *Shirley MacLaine Parker v. Twentieth Century-Fox Film Corp.*

Employees have a duty to mitigate, but only by seeking similar employment.

1. Facts:

    (a) August 6, 1965: Fox contracted with Parker to play the lead role in "Bloomer Girl" for $750,000, beginning May 23, 1966.

    (b) April 4, 1966: Fox told Parker that it was rescinding its offer for the lead role in "Bloomer Girl," but offered her another role in "Big Country, Big Man" for the same compensation.

2. Parker rejected the offer. She sued for money due and breach.

3. Fox admitted breach, but it argued that Parker could not recover because she failed to mitigate by declining the "Big Country" offer.

4. The trial court granted summary judgment for Parker.

5. Generally, employees must mitigate damages from their employers' breaches by seeking new employment, but the employment must be similar.

6. The court here held that the two films were not similar ("Bloomer Girl" was a musical and "Big Country" was a western). Affirmed.

### 5.2.4.7 *Punkar v. King Plastic Corp.*

1. A wrongfully discharged employee does not have to seek employment far from his home.

### 5.2.4.8 Reasonable Expenses in Mitigation: *Mr. Eddie, Inc. v. Ginsberg*

Reasonable expenses incurred in mitigation are compensable.

1. Mr. Eddie wrongfully discharged Ginsberg during a three-year employment contract. Ginsberg found a temporary job, where he earned $13,760. He then spent $1,340 unsuccessfully seeking more employment.

2. The court held that Ginsberg could recover the value of his original employment contract with Mr. Eddie, minus the $13,760 he earned at the second job, and plus the $1,340.

### 5.2.4.9 Mitigation through Inferior Employment: *Southern Keswick, Inc. v. Whetherholt*

1. If the discharged employee seeks inferior employment, his earnings should still be used in mitigation of damages.

### 5.2.4.10 Damages for Loss of Opportunity to Practice One's Profession

1. *Redgrave*: a plaintiff can recover for damages to his reputation if he can prove specific losses.[206]

2. English courts have allowed recovery for loss of opportunity to appear before the public, but American courts have not, absent evidence of specific losses.

## 5.2.5 Foreseeability

### 5.2.5.1 Reasonably Foreseeable Damages and Special Circumstances: *Hadley v. Baxendale*

1. A shaft broke at Hadley's mill. He contracted with Baxendale to ship it to the engineer to use as a model for a new shaft. Baxendale promised it could be shipped the next day, but in fact the shipment was delayed for several days. In the meantime, the mill was out of operation. Hadley sued for lost profits.

2. Held: Baxendale was unaware that the Mill couldn't operate without the shaft, and it was not a reasonable inference.

3. *First rule*: the party in breach is liable for reasonably foreseeable damages.

4. *Second rule*: if the party in breach is aware of special circumstances, he is liable for extra loss those circumstances create. But he is not liable for the extra loss if he was not aware of the special circumstances.

---

[206] Casebook pp. 276–77.

### 5.2.5.2 Commercial Breach: *Victoria Laundry (Windsor) Ltd. v. Newman Indus. Ltd.*

A commercial machine has only commercial uses. It's reasonably foreseeable that failing to deliver the machine will hinder commerce, especially when "the demand for laundry services at that time was insatiable."[207]

1. The plaintiff contracted to buy a bigger boiler for their laundry business. The defendant delayed delivery by more than five months. The plaintiff sued for lost profits.

2. The court held that the defendant should have known that the boiler would have been put into immediate commercial use. The plaintiff could recover because the lost profits were reasonably foreseeable damages resulting from breach.

3. Plaintiffs could not recover for "particularly lucrative contracts" it expected to procure, but they could still recover for "loss of business . . . to be reasonably expected."[208]

### 5.2.5.3 Market Fluctuations: *Koufos v. C. Czarnikow, Ltd. (The Heron II)*

1. The plaintiff chartered the defendant's ship to deliver a load of sugar. The defendant delayed shipment by nine days, during which the market price of sugar dropped.

2. Held: fluctuations in the price of sugar were reasonably foreseeable, so the shipper was liable for lost profits.

3. Lord Reid: a 25 percent change of an event occurring is reasonably foreseeable and thus compensable, but a 2 percent chance is not.

### 5.2.5.4 Commercial Machinery: *Hector Martinez & Co. v. Southern Pacific Transp. Co.*

"We must not lose sight of the basic common law rule, enunciated in *Hadley*, of damages for foreseeable loss."[209]

1. The plaintiff contracted with the defendant for the delivery of strip mining machinery. The defendant delayed shipment by a month.

2. Held: the plaintiff could recover for the rental value of the machinery for the month it was delayed. This case is distinct from *Hadley* in that commercial machinery has an obvious commercial use, while in *Hadley* it was not clear that the shaft was essential to the Mill's operation.

---

[207] Casebook p. 284.
[208] Casebook p. 285.
[209] Casebook p. 288.

## 5.2.5.5 The Scope of Hadley v. Baxendale

1. Courts usually apply *Hadley* to whether a given *type* of loss would be a reasonably foreseeable result of breach.

2. Courts also apply *Hadley* to determine the *amount* of loss—e.g., the court's holding in *Victoria Laundry* that the plaintiff could not recover for loss of particularly lucrative contracts because those contracts were not reasonably foreseeable.

3. But in *Wroth v. Tyler*, the defendant breached a contract to sell a house. After the breach, property values rose dramatically and unexpectedly. The court held the defendant was liable for the full difference, despite the unforeseeability of the damages amount.[210]

## 5.2.6 Certainty

1. Certainty applies in two ways:

    (a) **Causation**: it must be certain that the breach caused the loss.

    (b) **Amount**: to be compensable, the amount of loss must be certain.

### 5.2.6.1 *Kenford Co. v. Erie County*

To recover damages for lost profits, the plaintiff must show with certainty that the breach caused the alleged amount of loss.

1. Kenford and Dome contracted to build a stadium with Erie County. The parties were unable to negotiate a lease during the agreed one-year window, nor did construction ever begin. Kenford and Dome brought suit.

2. The trial court awarded the plaintiffs a multimillion-dollar jury verdict. The appellate court reversed lost profits damages and other expenses. The New York Court of Appeals heard only the issue of lost profits.

3. The New York standard for lost profits damages required (1) certainty that the breach caused the damages and (2) "the alleged loss must be capable of proof with reasonable certainty."[211] Damages must also have been within the contemplation of the parties when they made the contract.

4. The plaintiff's damages were not within the parties' contemplation and their projections, while sophisticated, are too remote (they rely only on the Astrodome). Reversed.

5. The court rejected the rational basis test from *Perma Research*, which allowed lost profits damages for new ventures if there was a "rational basis" for their calculation.[212]

---

[210]Casebook pp. 288–89.
[211]Casebook p. 293.
[212]Casebook pp. 294–95.

### 5.2.6.2 Ashland Management Inc. v. Janien

1. Ashland contracted with Janien to produce Eta, a sophisticated financial modeling tool. Ashland breached.

2. The court held that Janien could recover lost profits because they were not speculative—rather, the parties both believed the claims represented a fair forecast of future earnings, they were not entering an unfamiliar business, they had a "ready reservoir" of customers, and Eta had been extensively tested.

### 5.2.6.3 The New-Business Rule

1. Courts are wary of awarding speculative damages to new ventures. " ... the plaintiff must lay a basis for a reasonable estimate of the extent of his harm, measured in money."[213]

### 5.2.6.4 Consistency of Past Performance: *Rombola v. Cosindas*

1. Rombola agreed to maintain and race Cosinda's horse in exchange for 25% of the profits. Before a race, Cosindas took possession of the horse, depriving Rombola of the chance to win money.

2. The horse and Rombola had proved their ability to consistently win money. Rombola could recover consistent with their earlier performance.

### 5.2.6.5 Statistics of Similar Businesses: *Contemporary Mission, Inc. v. Famous Music Corp.*

1. Famous Music contracted with Contemporary Mission to produce records from the master tape of the rock opera *Virgin*. Famous Music failed to promote the records to Contemporary's satisfaction. The court held that statistical evidence of similarly-performing songs and albums in the past was admissible evidence to establish Contemporary's lost profits damages.

### 5.2.6.6 Uncertainty

1. *All or nothing rule*: one premise of *Kenford* is that there is some level of certainty above which the plaintiff can fully recover, and below which the plaintiff can recover nothing. This is wrong—the plaintiff should be compensated for the value of the *chance* to earn a profit, even if it is not certain that a profit would result.

2. Fuller and Eisenberg propose a formula for calculating damages based on probability based on the Capital Asset Pricing Model: damages should be awarded in proportion their likelihood. So if a venture has as 10% chance of $20 million and a 90% chance of $10 million, the award should be (0.10 x $20 million) + (0.90 x $10 million), or $11 million.

---
[213] Casebook pp. 296–97.

## 5.2.7 Liquidated Damages

### 5.2.7.1 Reasonable Approximation: *Wasserman's Inc. v. Middletown*

Liquidated damages clauses must reasonably approximate anticipated or actual damages.

1. Middletown entered into a commercial lease with Wasserman's for a tract of land the city owned. The contract provided that if Middletown cancelled the lease, it would reimburse Wasserman's for improvement costs and 25% of Wasserman's average gross receipts for a year.

2. Middletown later cancelled the lease but refused to pay damages as stipulated in the lease.

3. The trial court held that the agreement was enforceable. It awarded $346,058.44 to Wasserman's. Affirmed on appeal.

4. Middletown conceded the validity of the provision for reimbursement for improvements. Its sole claim was that the provision awarding 25% of receipts to Wasserman was an unenforceable penalty clause, rather than a valid liquidated damages clause.[214]

5. Liquidated damages clauses are unenforceable if they are punitive. To be valid, they must derive from "a good faith effort to estimate in advance the actual damages that will probably ensue from the breach . . . " [215]

6. The court here held that the liquidated damages provision did not necessarily reflect plaintiffs' actual losses. The other plaintiff, Jo-Ro (who had taken over the lease), had operated on a loss for the past year, despite the fact that its annual earnings since it first took the lease were $290,310.18.

7. Remanded to to the trial court to determine the reasonableness of the liquidated damages clause.

### 5.2.7.2 Provisions that Limit Damages

1. Underliquidated damages—an amount less than actual estimated damages—are usually enforced.

2. Other techniques include limiting liability for consequential damages or provisions that sellers' responsibilities are limited to replacing or repairing defective goods.

---

[214]Casebook p. 310.
[215]Casebook p. 311.

## 5.3 Specific Performance

### 5.3.0.3 Law & Equity

1. Common law distinction between law and equity:

   (a) *Law*: broadly, the principles for administering justice. Narrowly, the principles applied by common law courts.

   (b) *Equity*: broadly, fairness. Narrowly, the principles administered by equity courts. They did not have general jurisdiction. Rather, they existed to correct defects in common law court decisions.

2. Regarding contract law, the defect of common law courts was that they could not order specific performance. They could only award money damages. But equity courts could order specific performance (though sometimes they declined—e.g., if an opera singer breaches a contract, you don't want to force her to sing).[216]

3. Modern American courts have erased the law-equity structure, but judges and lawyers often preserve the mental distinction.

### 5.3.0.4 *London Bucket Co. v. Stewart*

Courts will generally not order specific performance when money damages are adequate (*but see Walgreen* below).

1. London Bucket Company contracted with a motel to install a heating system. The motel brought suit for breach, requesting specific performance "before the fall of cold weather."[217]

2. The trial court ordered specific performance. The appellate court reversed, holding that money damages would have adequately compensated the plaintiff for its injury.

3. "It is the general rule that contracts for building construction will not be specifically enforced because ordinarily damages are an adequate remedy and, in part, because of the incapacity of the court to superintend the performance."[218]

### 5.3.0.5 Injunction vs. Damages: *Walgreen Co. v. Sara Creek Property Co.*

1. Walgreen had a lease with Sara Creek to operate a pharmacy in a mall, with the promise that Walgreen would be the only pharmacy. Sara Creek wanted to lease a unit in the mall to Phar-Mor, which planned to operate a pharmacy equal in size to Walgreen. Walgreen sought an injunction.

---
[216]Casebook p. 325.
[217]Casebook p. 326.
[218]Casebook p. 327.

## 5 REMEDIES

2. Sara Creek argued that Walgreen's damages could be easily calculated. Walgreen argued that damages would be difficult to compute because they included intangibles like goodwill, so it sought an injunction.

3. The trial court awarded an injunction.

4. The choice of whether to award damages or an injunction rests on a cost-benefit analysis (for which the trial judge is responsible):

    (a) *Benefits of an injunction*:
    
    i. It shifts the burden of determining the costs of the defendant's conduct from the court to the parties.
    
    ii. " . . . prices and costs are more accurately determined by the market than by government."[219]
    
    (b) *Costs of an injunction*:
    
    i. It requires continuous court supervision.
    
    ii. It creates a "bilateral monopoly" in which two parties can only deal with each other.
    
    (c) *Benefits of damages*: avoid the costs of continuing supervision and bilateral monopoly.
    
    (d) *Costs of damages*: diminished accuracy in the determination of value, costs of litigation, costs of the court's time.
    
    (e) The only substantial cost of an injunction here would be prolonged negotiations, but that cost would be minimal, because Sara Creek could easily find a replacement for Phar-Mor.
    
    (f) The trial judge was correct to find that the cost of damages would exceed the cost of an injunction. Affirmed.

#### 5.3.0.6 Stokes v. Moore

1. An employment contract prevented Stokes from working in a similar line of business for a year if his current employment was terminated. It indicated that an injunction could prevent Stokes from pursuing similar work.

2. The court held that a contract cannot require an injunction, because the court has the sole discretion in deciding whether to issue an injunction.

#### 5.3.0.7 Uniqueness and Uncertainty: *Van Wagner Advertising Corp. v. S & M Enterprises*

Specific performance is appropriate when the value of property is uncertain, but not because the property is unique.

---
[219] Casebook p. 329.

1. Michaels leased advertising space on a building to Van Wagner with the understanding that Van Wagner would use it to build a sign. Michaels breached and Van Wagner sued for specific performance.

2. Van Wagner argued that specific performance was appropriate because of the "uniqueness" of the property. The court disagreed, holding that every piece of real property is unique. "The point at which breach of a contract will be redressable by specific performance thus must lie not in any inherent physical uniqueness of the property but instead in the uncertainty of valuing it . . ."[220]

## 5.4 The Reliance and Restitution Measures

### 5.4.1 Reliance Damages in a Bargain Context

#### 5.4.1.1 *Security Stove & Mfg. Co. v. American Rys. Express Co.*

When there are no measurable expectation damages, reliance damages may be the only way to avoid injustice.

1. Security Stove manufactured an oil and gas burner that it wanted to show at an exhibit on October 11th, 1926. American promised to deliver it by October 8th, but it didn't arrive until after the exhibition closed.

2. Security sued for reliance damages, including travel and exhibition expenses, totaling $801.51.

3. The court held that in general, when a shipper fails to deliver goods on time, the measure of damages should be the difference between the market value of the goods at the time promised and the market value of the goods at the time delivered.

4. But when the carrier knows that delay will cause "unusual loss," "the carrier is responsible for the real damage sustained from such delay . . ."[221]

5. Here, there were no lost profits, so awarding reliance damages would be the only way to avoid injustice.

#### 5.4.1.2 *Anglia Television Co. v. Reed*

1. Anglia planned to make a TV movie. It hired Robert Reed for £1,050. Reed breached and Anglia couldn't find a replacement, so it sued for out of pocket expenses of £2,000.

2. The court found for Anglia, holding that expenses made before the contract can be recovered under reliance damages if the breach caused them to be wasted.[222]

---

[220]Casebook p. 334.
[221]Casebook p. 342.
[222]Casebook p. 345.

### 5.4.1.3 *Beefy Trail, Inc. v. Beefy King Int'l, Inc.*

1. Usually, performance of a contract generates enough profit to cover expenditures. In case of breach, lost potential profits cannot be calculated with certainty, and courts should not award speculative damages. But expenditures can be measured with certainty, so courts should award reliance damages.

### 5.4.1.4 *L. Albert & Son v. Armstrong Rubber Co.*

1. The buyer wanted to buy a machine to recondition old rubber. It spent $3,000 building a foundation for the machine. The seller then breached.

2. The court held that the buyer should be able to recover reliance damages—but those damages should be offset if the seller can prove that the buyer's venture would not have been profitable enough to cover its expenses.

### 5.4.1.5 *C.C.C. Films (London) v. Impact Quadrant Films Ltd.*

1. When a plaintiff seeks reliance damages instead of expectation damages because the amount of lost profits were uncertain, who should bear the burden of proving whether the plaintiff would have had profits if the contract had been performed?

2. The court held that the defendant should bear the burden. If the plaintiff could not determine the amount of lost profits, it's also unlikely that the plaintiff would be able to determine whether profits would have been sufficient to cover expenditures.

### 5.4.1.6 *Westside Galvanizing Servs., Inc. v. Georgia-Pacific Corp.*

1. Georgia-Pacific wanted to build a chip-thickness screening facility. It contracted with Southeastern to supply steel, and Southeastern contracted with Westside to galvanize the steel.

2. Southeastern began defaulting on its contracts with both Westside and Georgia-Pacific. Westside stopped shipping the galvanized steel to Georgia-Pacific, but Georgia-Pacific persuaded it to ship the steel, promising payment.

3. Westside did not get paid, so it sued Georgia-Pacific for the amount due from Southeastern, arguing that it shipped the steel in reliance on Georiga-Pacific's promise that it would get paid.

4. The court held that Westside could sue Georgia-Pacific, but only for the value of the shipments made after the promise, not for all of Southeastern's obligation to Westside.

## 5.4.2 The Restitution Measure

### 5.4.2.1 *Osteen v. Johnson*

1. Johnson agreed to promote the plaintiffs' daughter, Linda Osteen, as a country singer and composer, including advertising, recording records, and sending records to DJs.

2. The trial court found that the defendant had substantially performed the agreement, but it awarded $1.00 plus costs "on the basis that the defendant had wrongfully caused the name of another party to appear on the label of the record as co-author of a song which had been written solely by Linda."[223]

3. On appeal, plaintiffs argued that damages were inadequate, and that the trial court wrongly concluded that the defendant had substantially performed the agreement.

4. The appellate court here held that restitution damages are appropriate when "the defendant's non-performance is so material that it is held to go to the "essence"" of the agreement.[224]

5. The court held that the defendant's breach was substantial. It remanded with the order to restore the plaintiffs' expenses of $2,500, minus the value of the services the defendant rendered.

### 5.4.2.2 Quantum Meruit: *United States v. Algernon Blair, Inc.*

Quantum meruit damages don't depend on the outcome of the contract.

1. Algernon Blair had a government construction contract. It subcontracted with Coastal. After Blair refused to pay for Coastal's crane rental, Coastal stopped working after finishing 28% of the job. The trial court found that Blair breached.

2. Coastal wanted to recover in quantum meruit for labor and equipment already furnished. Blair argued that if Coastal completed the contract, it would lose $37,000, so it would not be fair for Coastal to escape its loss by recovering in quantum meruit.

3. The court agreed with Coastal: "The impact of quantum meruit is to allow a promisee to recover the value of services he gave to the defendant irrespective of whether he would have lost money on the contract and been unable to recover in a suit on the contract."

---

[223] Casebook p. 348–49.
[224] Casebook p. 349.

## 5  REMEDIES

### 5.4.2.3  *Oliver v. Campbell*

Restitution damages are not available when parties have performed all of the contract except payment.

1. Campbell was divorcing his wife and hired Oliver as his lawyer for a fee of $850. At the end of the divorce proceedings, Campbell had paid Oliver $550 and refused to pay any more. Oliver brought suit to recover for the "reasonable value of his services," which the trial court found to be $5,000.

2. The court here held that Oliver should win $350. It refused to award restitution damages, holding that restitution is not available when the contract has been fully performed, and the only remaining performance is payment.

3. Judge Schauer, dissenting: the divorce case was likely to be appealed, and the contract would have continued, so damages should have included payment for counsel throughout the appeal.

### 5.4.2.4  G. Palmer, "The Law of Restitution"

1. When the contract has been fully performed and the only unfinished performance is payment, restitution is "regularly denied."[225] (*Oliver v. Campbell.*)

2. Meanwhile, if the contract is only partly performed, the promisee can recover restitution damages. This can lead to incongruous results when restitution damages exceed the contract price. (*Algernon Blair.*)

### 5.4.2.5  Restitution and Reliance Damages

1. " . . . restitutionary damages are based on *benefit conferred*, while reliance damages are based on *costs incurred.*"[226]

### 5.4.2.6  Expectation as a Cap on Reliance Damages

1. The majority rule (*Algernon Blair*) is that a promisee in an unprofitable contract can recover the market value of the benefit conferred, even if it exceeds the contract price. " . . . the expectation measure does not set a cap on restitutionary damages in a suit in unjust enrichment against a breaching promisor."[227]

2. What if the promisee sues for costs incurred, rather than benefit conferred? Will expectation damages set a cap?

---

[225] Casebook p. 353.
[226] Casebook p. 354.
[227] Casebook p. 354.

## 5   REMEDIES

(a) Restatement Second § 349: reliance damages are an alternative to expectation damages—but they should only apply when expectation damages are too uncertain or should be limited for other reasons.

(b) Reliance damages should not exceed the contract price.

### 5.4.2.7   Recovery for the Breaching Party: *Kutzin v. Pirnie*

"The Pirnies are entitled to restitution of their deposit less the amount of the injury to the Kutzins caused by the Pirnies' breach. To allow retention of the entire deposit would unjustly enrich the Kutzins and would penalize the Pirnies contrary to the policy behind our law of contracts."[228]

1. The defendants, the Pirnies, contracted to buy the house of the plaintiffs, the Kutzins, for $365,000. They put down a deposit of $36,000.

2. The contract included a provision which allowed an attorney to review the contract and give approval or disapproval within three days.

3. The Pirnies' lawyer wrote to cancel the contract. The Kutzins refused to return the deposit and sued for specific performance. The Pirnies counterclaimed for the return of their deposit. While the case was pending, the Kutzins sold the house for $352,500, so they amended their complaint to seek only $12,500 in damages (the difference between the sale price and the contract price), plus other incidental damages.

4. The trial court held the contract to be valid and awarded compensatory damages in an amount less than the deposit. It ordered the Kutzins to return the balance of the deposit after damages, or $18.675.

5. The appellate court held that the contract was binding but held that the sellers could keep the entire deposit.

6. Held:

    (a) The common law rule refused restitution damages when the party seeking damages was in breach, even if the seller had profited from the breach.

    (b) The modern trend (including in Restatement Second § 374(1)) is to allow recovery. If the seller retains the deposit but doesn't need it for compensation, the deposit becomes punitive.

    (c) The court affirmed the trial court's ruling.

---

[228] Casebook p. 362.

### 5.4.2.8 *United States Ex Rel. Palmer Const., Inc. v. Cal State Electric, Inc.*

1. What if a breaching party enriches the other, but gets nothing in return? That would create unjust enrichment and undue punishment. So, "the breaching party is entitled to the reasonable value of its services less any damages caused by the breach."[229]

### 5.4.2.9 *R.J. Berke & Co. v. Griffin, Inc.*

1. Should it matter for quantum meruit recovery whether the breach was willful?

### 5.4.2.10 *Vines v. Orchard Hills, Inc.*

1. The Vineses contracted to buy a condo from Orchard Hills for $78,800, for which they paid a deposit of $7,880. They later sought to recover the deposit after Mr. Vines' employer transferred him to New Jersey.

2. Recent cases allow restitution regardless of the cause of the breach. " . . . a party injured by breach of contract is entitled to retain nothing in excess of that sum which compensates him for the loss of his bargain."[230]

---

[229] Casebook p. 362.
[230] Casebook p. 364.

# § 6 Assent

## 6.1 Introduction to Interpretation

### 6.1.1 Subjectivity and Objectivity

1. Contracts generally require a "meeting of the minds."[231]

2. What happens in cases of misinterpretation? There's a tension between subjective and objective intent.

#### 6.1.1.1 Restatement First § 227

1. There are "six conceivable standards of interpretation":

    (a) General usage.

    (b) Limited usage—e.g., trade meaning.

    (c) Mutual usage—e.g., a meaning common to both parties, even if others don't follow the same meaning.

    (d) Individual usage—what the speaker intended, or, what the hearer understood.

    (e) Reasonable expectation—the meaning that the speaker reasonably should have expected his words to convey.

    (f) Reasonable understanding.

#### 6.1.1.2 Objective Intent: *Lucy v. Zehmer*

1. Lucy had been trying to buy Zehmer's farm. After a few drinks, Zehmer offered to sell for $50,000, and Lucy accepted. Zehmer wrote a contract on a napkin, had his wife sign it, and gave it to Lucy.

2. The court held that it "must look to the outward expression of a person as manifesting his intention rather than to his secret and unexpressed intention."[232] Even if Zehmer did not subjectively intend to sell the farm, his conduct gave rise to a reasonable interpretation that he did intend to sell. The court held that the sale contract was binding.

#### 6.1.1.3 *Keller v. Holderman*

1. No contract is made when "the whole transaction between the parties was a frolic and a banter."[233]

---

[231] Casebook p. 368.
[232] Casebook p. 373.
[233] Casebook p. 374.

## 6.1.1.4 Raffles v. Wichelhaus

1. Defendants agreed to buy cotton from the Plaintiffs from a ship named Peerless arriving at Liverpool from Bombay.

2. Another ship named Peerless arrived at Liverpool from Bombay. Defendants refused to pay because it was the wrong ship.

3. Multiple ships of the same name and origin created a "latent ambiguity." In light of that ambiguity, the court accepted evidence that the defendants meant one Peerless and the plaintiffs another. Held for the defendants.

## 6.1.1.5 Simpson, "Contracts for Cotton to Arrive: The Case of the Two Ships *Peerless*

1. At the time of *Raffles*, there were at least eleven ships named Peerless, so some confusion was understandable.

## 6.1.1.6 "Chicken": *Frigaliment Importing Co. v. B.N.S. Intern. Sales Co.*

1. "The issue is, what is chicken?"

2. The parties contracted for shipment of chicken, but they did not specify what type, and a dispute arose about whether the agreement meant young chicken, suitable for broiling and frying, or stewing chicken. The court looked to several sources to determine the meaning of "chicken," including the language of the contract, trade usage, and Department of Agriculture regulations.

3. The court ultimately held that the plaintiff failed to meet its burden of showing that it intended the narrower, rather than the broader, definition of chicken.

## 6.1.1.7 Oswald v. Allen

1. Oswald was interested in Mrs. Allen's coin collection. He agreed to buy her Swiss coins. He thought he had agreed to buy all of her Swiss coins. She thought she had agreed to sell only her Swiss Coin Collection, and not the other Swiss coins in her Rarity Coin Collection.

2. The court held that this case was "within the small group of exceptional cases in which there is 'no sensible basis for choosing between conflicting understandings.'"

## 6.1.1.8 Falck v. Williams

1. The parties used a code for business communications. After an ambiguous communication, the plaintiff sued for breach of contract. The court held for the defendant on the ground that neither party's interpretation was the true one.

# 6 ASSENT

### 6.1.1.9 Colfax Envelope Corp. v. Local No. 458-3M

1. "If neither party can be assigned the greater blame for the misunderstanding, there is no nonarbitrary basis for deciding which party's understanding to enforce, so the parties are allowed to abandon the contract without liability."[234]

### 6.1.1.10 Intent: *Embry v. Hargadine, McKittrick Dry Goods Co.*

Contracts generally require a meeting of the minds, but intent is irrelevant if the other party could not reasonably know the other's intent.

1. Embry supported the company's sales team. After his one-year contract was up, Embry tried to get McKittrick to agree to another contract. After a brief conversation in McKittrick's office where McKittrick said, "Go ahead, you're all right. Get your men out . . . "[235] Embry understood his words as assenting to a new one-year contract. McKittrick didn't.

2. The key issue was whether both parties intended to create a contract.

3. Contracts generally require a meeting of the minds, but intent is irrelevant if the other party could not reasonably know the other's intent.

4. Held for Embry.

### 6.1.1.11 CISG and Intent: *MCC-Marble Ceramic Center, Inc. v. Ceramica Nuova D'Agostino*

CISG allows the court to discern the parties' subjective intent, even absent outward manifestations.

Would this case have come out differently if US law controlled?

1. MCC contracted to buy tiles from D'Agostino. They signed a form contract.

2. MCC brought suit for D'Agostino's failure to fill orders. D'Agostino argued that it was not obligated to fill the orders because MCC had defaulted on earlier payments.

3. The form contract gave D'Agostino the right to cancel if MCC failed to pay. MCC argued that it failed to pay because some of the tiles were unsatisfactory—but the contract also had a clause requiring written notice of complaints, which MCC did not give.

4. MCC argued that it had an oral agreement with D'Agostino that the clauses in the form contract would not apply.

---

[234]Casebook p. 381.
[235]Casebook p. 382.

## 6  ASSENT

5. CISG allows inquiry into subjective intent, "even if the parties did not engage in any objectively ascertainable means of registering this intent."[236]

6. Three affiants testified to MCC's intent to nullify the clauses. While the affidavits may have been conclusory, they at least presented a triable issue of fact, so summary judgment was inappropriate.

### 6.1.1.12  Mayol v. Weiner Companies, Ltd.

1. Mayol contracted to buy a piece of property which Weiner sold on behalf of the owner. The contract included a clause granting possession "on or before November 1, 1979 subject to tenant's rights." Mayol paid a $1,000 deposit.

2. It turned out that the tenant had a right to purchase. Upon learning this, Mayol breached and sued to recover his deposit.

3. Mayol had asked about the lease but Weiner had not told him about the tenant's purchase option until after the sale contract was complete. The court held for Mayol, reasoning that he had no reason to believe that he was buying property subject to a purchase option, and the seller had no reason to think that Mayol believed so, either.

### 6.1.1.13  Objective and Subjective Elements in Interpretation

1. Classical contract law largely disregarded the parties' intent.

2. There are four principles of interpretation in modern contract law:[237]

    (a) The more reasonable meaning prevails If both parties attach different subjective meanings to an expression and they are not equally reasonable.

    (b) But if the two meanings are equally reasonable, neither prevails.

    (c) If the parties attach the same meaning, that meaning prevails even if it is unreasonable.

    (d) If A and B attach different meanings, and A knows B's meaning but B doesn't know A's, B's meaning prevails even if it is less reasonable.

### 6.1.1.14  Berke Moore Co. v. Phoenix Bridge Co.

1. Mutual understanding is not private and is therefore valid.

---

[236] Casebook p. 387.
[237] Casebook p. 394–95.

6 ASSENT 122

### 6.1.2 Problems of Interpreting Purposive Language

#### 6.1.2.1 Fish, "Normal Circumstances, Literal Language, Direct Speech Acts, the Ordinary, the Everyday, the Obvious, What Goes Without Saying, and Other Special Cases"

1. There is no single, literal meaning of a phrase.[238]

#### 6.1.2.2 *Haines v. New York*

1. The parties disagreed over whether New York City had an obligation to expand a sewage system arising from a much earlier agreement.

2. " . . . where the parties have not clearly expressed the duration of a contract, the courts will imply that they intended performance to continue for a reasonable time."[239]

#### 6.1.2.3 *Spaulding v. Morse*

1. A divorce agreement included a promise by Morse to pay his son $1,200 per year until he entered college. His son was drafted into the army and tried to enforce the agreement.

2. The court held that Morse did not have to pay. The court held that it should take "material circumstances" into account to honor the parties' intent.

#### 6.1.2.4 *Lawson v. Martin Timber Co.*

1. Lawson and Martin agreed that Lawson could cut timber from Martin's land for two years, but in the event of high water, Lawson could get a one-year extension. Lawson continued to cut after the two year period. Martin sued.

2. There had been high water during the two year period. The court held for Martin.

3. The dissent argued that the parties intended the extension to take effect only if high water *prevented* Lawson from harvesting the timber. But in fact it only prevented him from harvesting for half the time. During the other half, he could have easily harvested the lumber.

#### 6.1.2.5 Lieber, "Legal and Political Hermeneutics"

1. Some amount of interpretation is always necessary—e.g., "fetch some soupmeat."[240]

---

[238] Casebook pp. 398–99.
[239] Casebook p. 401.
[240] Casebook p. 405.

# 6 ASSENT

### 6.1.3 Usage, Course of Dealing, and Course of Performance

#### 6.1.3.1 Trade Usage: *Foxco Industries, Ltd. v. Fabric World, Inc.*

1. The parties disagreed over the meaning of the term "first quality goods." The court, following UCC 2-202(a), held that the trade usage applied.[241]

#### 6.1.3.2 Trade Quantities: *Hurst v. W.J. Lake & Co.*

1. "Minimum 50% protein" included levels of 49.5% protein, just as "a thousand bricks" only means a wall of a certain size, and 4,000 shingles can really mean 2,500.

#### 6.1.3.3 *Flower City Painting Contractors, Inc. v. Gumina*

1. Flowers, unaware of trade usage, thought it had only contracted to paint the interior of the building. The court held that the fundamental difference in intent meant that there was no contract. *Raffles v. Wichelhaus.*

#### 6.1.3.4 J. White & R. Summers, UCC § 1-2

1. The UCC defines "agreement" to include "implications from other circumstances," including trade usage, thus broadening the definition of contract.

## 6.2 Offer and Revocation

### 6.2.1 What Constitutes an Offer

#### 6.2.1.1 *Lonergan v. Scolnick*

1. There is an important distinction between intent to find out if the other party is interested and intent to make a definite offer.[242]

#### 6.2.1.2 *Regent Lighting Corp. v. CMT Corp.*

1. If a party reserves the right to not accept an offer, a proposal is only an invitation to submit an offer.

#### 6.2.1.3 Unilateral Offer: *Lefkowitz v. Great Minneapolis Surplus Store*

1. Great Minneapolis published a newspaper ad naming prices for goods on a "first come, first served" basis. Lefkowitz arrived first, but Great Minneapolis refused to sell to him because he was not a woman.

2. Lefkowitz argued that the ad constituted a unilateral offer.

---

[241] Casebook pp. 407–08.
[242] Casebook p. 416.

3. A binding obligation arises from newspaper ads if "the facts show that some performance was promised in positive terms for something requested."[243] "... where the offer is clear, definite, and explicit, and leaves nothing open for negotiation, it constitutes an offer, acceptance of which will complete the contract."[244]

### 6.2.1.4 Limits on Unilateral Offer: *Ford Motor Credit Co. v. Russell*

1. An ad offered 11% financing on a car. Russell only qualified for %13.75 financing. He defaulted. He argued that the ad constituted an offer.

2. The court held that it was not an offer because not everyone would qualify for the 11% financing and the dealership did not have an unlimited number of cars to sell.

### 6.2.1.5 *Donovan v. RRL Corp.*

1. Is a newspaper ad an offer or an invitation to negotiate? Courts generally hold that it is an offer if it **requires the consumer to perform a specific act** (e.g., first come, first served). But does that align with consumers' reasonable expectations? Does traveling to the store count as an act?

### 6.2.1.6 *Fisher v. Bell*

1. Displaying something in a shop window with a price tag is an invitation, not an offer.

### 6.2.1.7 Auctions for Sale of Land: *Hoffman v. Horton*

1. UCC § 2-328 allows an auctioneer to reopen bidding if someone announces a bid while his hammer is falling. This rule should apply to land auctions.

### 6.2.1.8 Auctions

1. Reserve rules allow auctioneers to withhold sales if the highest bid is too low. This may seem wrong to casual auctiongoers, but it is "unlikely to frustrate the expectations of most bidders."[245]

### 6.2.1.9 Note on Offer and Acceptance

1. People are not legally bound when they make appointments or reservations.[246]

---

[243]Williston. Casebook p. 418.
[244]Casebook p. 419.
[245]Casebook p. 423.
[246]Casebook p. 424.

## 6.2.2 Lapse, Rejection, and Counter-Offer

### 6.2.2.1 *Akers v. J.B. Sedberry, Inc.*

1. In a meeting, Akers offered to resign. Sedberry said she would not accept the resignation.

2. Several days later, she sent Akers a telegram accepting his resignation.

3. "An offer may be terminated in a number of ways, as, for example, where it is rejected by the offeree, or where it is not accepted by him within the time fixed, or, if no time is fixed, within a reasonable time. An offer terminated in either of these ways ceases to exist and cannot therefore be accepted."[247]

4. Did the offer to resign extend beyond the in-person meeting? The court held that it did not.

### 6.2.2.2 *Effect of the Rejection of an Offer*

1. When does an offeree terminate his power of acceptance?

2. Generally, it's when the offeror would reasonably understand that the offeree has taken the offer off the table.

### 6.2.2.3 Qualified vs. Absolute Acceptance: *Ardente v. Horan*

A qualified acceptance, subject to a condition, does not create a contractual obligation if the other party does not satisfy the condition.

1. Ardente tried to buy property from Horan. He sent a $20,000 deposit with a letter asking the sellers to leave behind certain furnishings (patio furniture, etc.). Horan declined and returned the deposit. Ardente sued for specific performance.

2. The issue was whether Ardente's deposit and letter constituted a contract, hinging on the condition in the letter. Was it a qualified acceptance, subject to a condition, or an "absolute acceptance together with a mere inquiry concerning a collateral matter"?[248]

3. The court held that Ardente's letter was a qualified acceptance, binding only if Horan met its conditions. Thus, "it operated as a rejection of the defendants' offer and no contractual obligation was created."[249]

---

[247] Casebook p. 427.
[248] Casebook p. 432.
[249] Casebook p. 432.

### 6.2.2.4 Benficial Condition: *Rhode Island Dep't of Transp. v. Providence & Worcester R.R.*

1. A state statute provided that if a railroad sold land, the state had an option to purchase at the price of the lowest offer. Providence & Worcester were selling a piece of land. They had an offer from Promet for $100,000, which included a promise from Providence to remove all railroad tracks.

2. The state exercised its purchase option, but told Providence that it could leave the tracks. Providence argued that there was no contract because the state's response was a conditional acceptance.

3. The court held for the state because the state's response "did not add any terms or conditions to the contract but, instead, constituted a clear benefit to P & W."[250] In fact, it *released* Providence from an obligation.

### 6.2.2.5 Grumbling Acceptance: *Price v. Oklahoma College of Osteopathic Medicine and Surgery*

1. A professor accepted an employment offer but added a note protesting the terms.

2. "The notation amounted to no more than saying I don't like your offer, I don't think it's right or fair, but I accept it. That and nothing more."[251]

### 6.2.2.6 Mirror-Image Rule

1. Under classical contract law, the **mirror image rule** held that no contract was formed if the acceptance differed from the offer in any way. Modern contract law has softened the rule in two ways:

    (a) UCC § 2-207—see below.

    (b) Restatement Second § 59: an acceptance containing additional terms is binding if acceptance does not depend on the offeror's assent to the additional terms.

### 6.2.2.7 Renewal by Implication: *Livingstone v. Evans*

1. A seller can renew an offer by implication.

2. For instance—S: I'll sell for $1,800. B: How about $1,600? S: Sorry, can't go any lower. B: Ok, then, $1,800.

3. S renewed the offer by implication. The contract is binding.

---

[250] Casebook p. 433.
[251] Casebook p. 435.

## 6 ASSENT

#### 6.2.2.8  Culton v. Gilchrist

1. A tenant renewed his lease. When he renewed, he asked if he could add a cookroom to the house. The court held that the landlord's acceptance of the offer did not depend on the cookroom.

### 6.2.2.9  Effect of the Offeror's Death or Incapacity Before Acceptance

1. The traditional rule is that the death or incapacity of the offeror terminates the offeree's power of acceptance if the offer was revocable when the death or incapacity occurred.[252]

2. The rule mainly applies when the decedent offeror's estate is not excused from performance.

3. Eisenberg suggests that a better rule would be that the offeree in this case should be able to recover reliance damages, but not expectation damages.[253]

### 6.2.3  Revocation

#### 6.2.3.1  What Constitutes Receipt of Written Acceptance?

1. Receipt happens when the person conducting the transaction receives it or "when it would have been brought to his attention if the organization had exercised due diligience . . ."[254]

#### 6.2.3.2  Preparing for Performance: *Ragosta v. Wilder*

1. The plaintiffs wanted to buy "The Fork Shop" from the defendants. The defendants rejected the plaintiffs' initial offer, but responded with a counteroffer, offering to sell at $88,000 anytime until November 1 unless another buyer came along.

2. On October 1, the plaintiffs called the defendants to tell them they accepted the offer. On October 6, the plaintiffs called to say they would come on October 10 to close the deal.

3. On October 8, the defendants called to say that they were no longer willing to sell.

4. The plaintiffs sued for specific performance.

5. The trial court held for the plaintiffs, finding that (1) the plaintiffs had accepted the defendants' offer and (2) the plaintiffs had relied on the offer and had begun performance by securing financing.

---
[252] Casebook p. 436.
[253] Casebook p. 438.
[254] Casebook p. 442.

6. The court here reversed, holding that the defendants' promise to keep the offer open unless another buyer came along was not binding because there had been no consideration.

7. Obtaining financing did not constitute consideration. It was preparation for performance, not performance itself.

8. However, the court allowed the plaintiffs to recover reliance damages under promissory estoppel.

### 6.2.3.3 Offers for Unilateral Contracts

1. Under classical contract law, the **unilateral contract rule** held that an offer "could be revoked at any time before the designated act had been completed, even if performance of the act had begun."[255]

2. This rule frustrated the parties' expectations and defied the interests of offerors as a class.[256]

3. So, the Restatement (First) drew a distinction between *performing* and *preparing to perform*, which the court followed in *Ragosta v. Wilder*. But the distinction can be hard to justify. For instance, say the unilateral offer is that I'll give you $1,000 to cross the Brooklyn Bridge. If you take one step on the bridge, there is a contract. But if you spend hours preparing, there is no contract.

### 6.2.3.4 Reliance and Revocability: *Drennan v. Star Paving Co.*

Promissory estoppel prevents a subcontractor from revoking its offer once the contractor has acted upon the subcontractor's promise.

1. Facts:

    (a) Drennan was preparing a bid for a school construction job. His final bid was $317,385. He had to provide a 10% bond as a guarantee that he would enter the contract.

    (b) On July 28, 1955 Drennan received between 50 and 75 subcontractor bids. Star Paving Co. put in a bid for $7,131.60 for paving work.

    (c) Drennan's was the winning bid. The next day, he stopped by Star Paving's offices, where one of its engineers told him they had mistakenly underbid. The had intended to bid $15,000 and refused to do the job for anything less.

    (d) Drennan found another company, L & H, to do the paving for $10,948.60. Drennan then sued Star for the difference, or $3,817.00.

---

[255] Casebook p. 446.
[256] Casebook pp. 446–47.

2. Star argued that "there was no enforceable contract between the parties on the ground that it made a revocable offer and revoked it before plaintiff communicated his acceptance to defendant."[257]

3. Drennan argued that "he relied to his detriment on defendant's offer and that defendant must therefore answer in damages for its refusal to perform."

4. The trial court held that Star made a definite offer and that Drennan relied on Star's bid in computing his own bid. It awarded $3,817.00 in reliance damages to Drennan.

5. Earlier cases held that the subcontractor is not bound because there was no binding promise of an irrevocable offer and no consideration.

6. On appeal, the question was whether Drennan's reliance made Star's offer irrevocable.

7. Judge Traynor:

    (a) Star's offer was a promise. Since Star was silent on revocation, the court had to decide whether the promise was revocable.

    (b) Restatement § 90 hold that justifiable reliance can make a promise binding, even absent bargained-for consideration.[258]

    (c) Star should have known that Drennan would have relied on its promise in computing its bid—indeed, it wanted him to.[259]

    (d) Star also argued that its bid was the result of a mistake, so it was entitled to revoke it. The court held that it would be revocable only if Drennan had not relied on it. But here, Star's mistake misled Drennan, causing further detriment and creating an additional reason to enforce the promise.

    (e) Star's last argument was that Drennan failed to mitigate damages. The court dismissed this argument, finding that he had.

### 6.2.3.5 Critiques of *Drennan*: *Pavel Enterprises, Inc. v. A.S. Johnson Co. 452*

1. Subcontractors are bound to the general, but the general is not bound to the subcontractor, creating incentives for the general contractor to act unethically:

    (a) *Bid shopping*: using the lowest bid to negotiate lower bids from others.

---

[257]Casebook p. 449.
[258]Casebook p. 450. This case was decided in 1958. The ALI published the Restatement in 1932 and Restatement Second in 1979.
[259]Casebook p. 450–51.

# 6 ASSENT

(b) *Bid chopping*: pressuring the subcontractor to make a lower bid.

(c) *Bid peddling*: a subcontractor waits until other bids are in and then undercutting them, avoiding the cost of estimating his own bid.

2. Most courts have followed *Drennan*, but at least one has deviated.[260]

### 6.2.3.6 Dodge, "Teaching the CISG in Contracts"

1. Common law: "an offer is freely revocable, even if the offeror has promised to hold it open, unless that promise is supported by consideration or reliance."[261]

2. UCC: merchants can make a "firm offer" (i.e., an irrevocable offer) without the need for consideration. The offeror must be a merchant, etc.[262]

3. CISG Art. 16 allows an offeror to make an irrevocable offer without these restrictions.

### 6.2.3.7 Limiting *Drennan*: *Preload Technology, Inc. v. A.B. & J. Construction Co., Inc.*

1. When the general contractor engages in the practices warned against in *Pavel Enterprises* (bid shopping, etc.), § 90 reliance may not be available.

### 6.2.3.8 Restatement Second § 87(2): Option Contract

1. "An offer which the offeror should reasonably expect to induce action or forbearance of a substantial character on the part of the offence before acceptance and which does induce such action or forbearance is binding as an option contract to the extent necessary to avoid injustice."

2. An option contract is an offer in which the offeror promises to keep the offer open for a certain period of time. For instance, a seller grants a buyer the option to buy his house for $1,000 anytime during the next month.

3. The distinction between §§ 45 and 87 is that an offeree who has begun performance can recover expectation damages, while an offeree who has not begun performance can only recover reliance damages.[263]

---

[260] Casebook p. 453.
[261] Casebook p. 453.
[262] Casebook p. 453.
[263] Casebook p. 455.

6 ASSENT

## 6.3 Modes of Acceptance

### 6.3.1 Acceptance by Act

#### 6.3.1.1 Promise to Bequeath: *Klockner v. Green*

A promise becomes binding when the offeree acts on the offeror's request.

1. Richard and Francis Klockner were stepson and stepgranddaughter of the decedent, Edyth Klockner. Edith Klockner left a will devising her property to her husband, who predeceased her, so upon her death her property would have passed to her heirs by the rules of intestate succession.

2. However, Edyth Klockner promised to leave her real property to Richard and her personal property to Francis. She had her attorney draw up a will to this effect, but she never signed it—"stymied by her own superstition."[264]

3. Richard and Francis testified that they would have taken care of Edyth even if she hadn't promised to leave them her property. The trial court held that there was no contract because there was no offer and acceptance nor consideration. The appellate court held that the statute of frauds barred enforcement because there had been no reliance.

    (a) Statute of frauds: at common law, it held that contracts are not enforceable if they are not in writing.

4. The question on appeal was whether Edyth Klockner entered into a valid, binding contract with Richard and Francis to bequeath her property to them.

5. Held: Edyth's promise became binding when Richard and Francis acted upon it. It need not have been their sole motivation. Edyth also received the benefit of her bargain.

#### 6.3.1.2 Diamond Jim: *Simmons v. United States*

1. A brewery tagged a fish named Diamond Jim III. It promised a $25,000 reward to anyone who caught it.

2. Simmons caught Diamond Jim III. He knew about the contest, but he also knew that his chances of catching this particular fish were minuscule, and "he did not have the fish in mind when he set out to go fishing."[265]

3. The IRS taxed the prize as income. Simmons claimed it was a gift.

---

[264]Casebook p. 464.
[265]Casebook p. 466.

# 6  ASSENT

4. The court held that an offer for a prize or reward is an offer for a unilateral contract. "For the offer to be accepted the contract to become binding, the desired act must be performed with knowledge of the offer." "So long as the outstanding offer was known to him, a person may accept an offer for a unilateral contract by rendering performance, even if he does so primarily for reasons unrelated to the offer."[266]

5. Held: the prize was income.

### 6.3.1.3  *Stephens v. Memphis*

1. Payment of rewards shouldn't be based on knowledge of the reward. Do we want people to avoid doing their civic duty unless they know they'll get paid?

### 6.3.1.4  Performance of a Condition as Acceptance: *Carlill v. Carbolic Smoke Ball, Inc.*

Performing a condition counts as acceptance of the offer. For instance, if the Carbolic Smoke Ball manufacturers promise a reward for anyone who uses the product and gets sick, anyone who performs those conditions has accepted the offer and can recover the reward.

1. The manufacturers of "The Carbolic Smoke Ball" placed a newspaper ad promising a cash reward for anyone who became sick after using their product three times daily for two weeks. The plaintiff did and got sick. She sued for the reward.

2. The trial court held that she could recover the value of the reward.

3. Was this a promise or "mere puff"?[267] It was a promise.

4. Was it binding? The defendants argued that the promise was made to nobody in particular. The court held that the ad was an offer to pay the reward to "anyone who will perform these conditions, and the performance of the conditions is the acceptance of the offer."[268]

5. The defendants also argued that there was no notice requirement. The court held that notice was irrelevant.

6. The defendants argued, finally, that there was no consideration. The court disagreed, finding that any use of their product conferred a benefit. Moreover, consumers are inconvenienced when they use the Carbolic Smoke Ball.

7. Affirmed.

---

[266]Casebook p. 466.
[267]Casebook p. 467.
[268]Casebook p. 467.

# 6 ASSENT

### 6.3.2 Subjective Acceptance

#### 6.3.2.1 *International Filter Co. v. Conroe Gin, Ince, & Light Co.*

1. International Filter manufactured water purifying machinery. Conroe made ice, etc. International Filter sent Conroe a proposal for the sale of two water tanks. The proposal dictated that it "becomes a contract when accepted by the purchaser and approved by an executive officer of International Filter Company ..."[269]

2. Conroe wrote back with "Accepted." The president of International Filter wrote "O.K." International then sent Conroe a confirmation.

3. Conroe later tried to back out. International Filter sued for performance.

4. Conroe argued (1) that International's "O.K." did not amount to an approval by an executive and (2) that International did not notify Conroe of its acceptance of the contract.[270]

5. The trial court found for Conroe. Affirmed on appeal.

6. The court here held that International was not required to communicate its acceptance. As long as an executive at International approved the order, notice of the approval to Conroe was not necessary.

7. Moreover, even if notice had been required (which it wasn't), International's "O.K." would have been good enough.

8. Reversed.

### 6.3.3 Acceptance by Conduct

#### 6.3.3.1 Regular Conduct as Tacit Assent: *Polaroid Corp. v. Rollins Environmental Services (NJ), Inc.*

1. Rollins operated a hazardous waste disposal facility. Rollins disposed of hazardous waste from Polaroid and Occidental.

2. Hazardous waste disposal agreements between Polaroid/Occidental and Rollins included an indemnification for liability for spills. Occidental included its indemnity clause in its purchase orders. Rollins accepted these purchase orders several times before it objected.

3. Polaroid and Occidental sued for a determination that Rollins was obligated to indemnify them against liability for hazardous waste spills.

4. The trial court held that Polaroid and Occidental had valid contracts with Rollins indemnifying them from liability.

---

[269] Casebook p. 471.
[270] Casebook p. 472.

# 6 ASSENT

5. The New Jersey Department of Environmental Protection requested compensation of $9,224,189 for cleanup.

6. Rollins argued that it was not obligated to indemnify Occidental because it refused the purchase orders containing the indemnity clause. The court here disagreed, holding that Rollins had silently assented to the terms of the contract. " . . . when an offeree accepts the offeror's services without expressing any objections to the offer's essential terms, the offeree has manifested assent to those terms."[271]

7. Affirmed.

## 6.3.4 The Effect of Using a Subcontractor's Bid

### 6.3.4.1 *Holman Erection Co. v. Orville E. Madsen & Sons, Inc.*

1. Madsen was a general contractor. Holman submitted a bid as a subcontractor, which Madsen included in its general bid. Madsen won the bid and awarded the subcontract to a different company. Holman sued for lost profits, arguing that inclusion of Holman's bid in Madsen's general bid created a binding contract.

2. The trial court held that there had been no contract. It granted Madsen's motion for summary judgment.

3. "Does the act of listing Holman in the general bid constitute an acceptance of Holman's offer to do the work when no other communication occurred after the offer and prior to the substitution of a different subcontractor? We think not."[272]

4. Holman argued that listing it as a subcontract counted as acceptance because (1) there is no other reasonable explanation, (2) it is unfair to bind Holman without binding Madsen, and (3) Madsen knew that its general bid was public record, so it should have expected that Holman would have seen it.

5. The court considered several reasons for binding general contractors to subcontractors upon listing their bids,[273] but ultimately held that the justifications for "unequal treatment of generals and subcontractors" were more persuasive.[274]

6. Affirmed.

---
[271] Casebook p. 478.
[272] Casebook p. 480.
[273] Casebook p. 482.
[274] Casebook p. 483.

### 6.3.4.2 *Southern California Acoustics, Inc. v. C.V. Holder, Inc.*

1. The statute underlying *Holman* was later amended to prevent general contractors from substituting subcontractors unless the subcontractor was unable or unwilling to perform.[275]

### 6.3.5 Silence As Acceptance

#### 6.3.5.1 *Vogt v. Madden*

1. Vogt had an oral sharecrop agreement with Madden to farm Madden's land in 1979 and 1980. The issue was whether there was an agreement to farm the land in 1981. The crops had been doing poorly. Vogt proposed growing beans. Madden did not respond. Vogt took Madden's silence as an acceptance. Madden did not, and he leased the land to another tenant for 1981.

2. The trial court held for Vogt.

3. Can silence constitute acceptance?

    (a) By default, silence does not constitute acceptance.

    (b) Restatement Second § 69 recognizes two exceptions: (1) when the offeree silently takes offered benefits and (2) "where one party relies on the other party's manifestation of intention that silence may operate as acceptance."[276]

    (c) Neither exception applied here.

4. Madden's silence was not assent, so there was no contract. Reversed.

#### 6.3.5.2 *Laurel Race Courses v. Regal Const. Co.*

1. Laurel hired Regal to build a track. After a dispute about quality, Regal did extra work.

2. Regal claimed that it reached an agreement with Laurel that Regal would absorb the cost of the extra work if Regal's defective workmanship caused it, but otherwise Laurel would pay Regal on a cost-plus basis. Laurel replied to this proposal with silence. Regal then did the extra work.

3. Did Laurel's silence count as assent?

4. The court held that it did, recognizing an exception to the general rule that silence does not count as acceptance. "Where the offeree with reasonable opportunity to reject offered services takes the benefit of them under circumstances which would indicate to a reasonable person that they were offered with the expectation of compensation, he assents to the term proposed and thus accepts the offer."[277]

---

[275]Casebook p. 485.
[276]Casebook p. 493.
[277]Casebook p. 495.

### 6.3.5.3 Cole-McIntyre-Norfleet Co. v. Holloway

1. A traveling salesman sold to 50 barrels of meal to a store. The meal didn't arrive. When the store inquired, the sales company told him that it had rejected his order without telling him, so there was no contract.

2. The contract provided that it was not binding until the company's office in Memphis accepted the order.

3. The lower court held that the delay in rejection counted as acceptance.

4. The court here affirmed. "It will not do to say that a seller of goods like these could wait indefinitely to decide whether or not he will accept the offer of the proposed buyer."[278]

### 6.3.5.4 Duty to Promptly Reply: Kukusa v. Home Mut. Hail-Tornado Ins. Co.

1. Kukusa applied for insurance to protect his crops from hail. After two months, he received a rejection. That afternoon, his crops suffered severe hail damage.

2. The court held for Kukusa. If the insurance company had not unreasonably delayed, Kukusa could have acquired other insurance before the hailstorm. The insurance company had a duty to promptly reply.

### 6.3.5.5 Standing Offer: Hobbs v. Massasoit Whip Co.

1. Repeated orders for the same product can count as a standing offer. If the buyer does not reject future shipments, his silence counts as acceptance.[279]

### 6.3.5.6 Louisville Tin & Stove Co. v. Lay

1. Taking physical control of shipped goods counts as acceptance of the shipment.

### 6.3.5.7 Austin v. Burge

1. The defendant had a two year newspaper subscription. After the subscription period had ended, the newspaper kept sending him the paper. He paid the bills twice, but both times he asked to cancel the subscription.

2. The court held for the newspaper, finding that the defendant had continued to enjoy the benefit of the newspaper, so he had an obligation to pay for it.

---

[278] Casebook p. 497.
[279] Casebook p. 499.

## 6 ASSENT

### 6.3.5.8 Negative-Option Plans

1. A **negative-option** plan involves a subscription for merchandise, like a book or record club. They differ from unordered goods in that the customer contracts in advance.

### 6.3.5.9 The Significance of Unjust Enrichment and Loss through Reliance in Cases Where Silence Is Treated as Acceptance

1. After receiving an offer, there are three kinds of silence:

    (a) The offeree silently appropriates the benefit.

    (b) The offeror changes his position by (1) assuming the offer has been accepted or (2) forgoing other opportunities (*Kukusa*).

    (c) There is no enrichment or detrimental reliance, but the offeror forms an expectation of profit on the offeree's silence.

### 6.3.6 Acceptance by Electronic Agent

1. VETA and E-Sign have clarified that electronic records and signatures satisfy the statute of frauds.

2. Contracts can be formed between a person and a computer, or even between two computers.[280] " ... it is conceivable that, with the useful life of this Act, electronic agents may be created with the ability to act autonomously, and not just automatically."[281]

## 6.4 Implied-in-Law and Implied-in-Fact Contracts; Unilateral Contracts Revisited

### 6.4.1 Contract Implied in Law: *Nursing Care Services, Inc. v. Dobos*

1. Dobos was admitted to the hospital for an abdominal aneurysm. The doctor ordered around-the-clock nursing care. She ended up receiving nursing care for (1) two weeks in the hospital, (2) 48 hours of post-release care, and (3) two weeks of at-home care. The total bill was $3,723.90. Dobos contested periods (1) and (3).

2. The court held that the Nursing Care Services failed to establish an express contract or a contract implied in fact. But it did establish a contract implied in law.

---

[280] Casebook p. 502.
[281] Casebook p. 503.

# 6 ASSENT

3. "Contracts implied in law, or as they are more commonly called 'quasi contracts,' are obligations imposed by law on grounds of justice and equity. Their purpose is to prevent unjust enrichment. Unlike express contracts or contracts implied in fact, quasi contracts do not rest upon the assent of the contracting parties."[282]

4. The **officious intermeddler** doctrine prevents foisting labor upon another without consent. But the **emergency aid exception** allows recovery if the intervener "acted unofficiously and with intent to charge . . ."[283]

### 6.4.2 *Sceva v. True*

1. The implied contract is "doubtless a legal fiction, invented and used for the sake of the remedy. If it was originally usurpation, certainly it has now become very inveterate, and firmly fixed in the body of law."[284]

### 6.4.3 Implied-in-Fact and Implied-in-Law Contracts

1. **Implied-in-fact** contracts are true contracts in which assent is implied, not explicit—e.g., raising your hand to bid at an auction.[285]

2. **implied-in-law** contracts arise from liability for unjust enrichment. See *Nursing Care Services, Inc. v. Dobos* above.

### 6.4.4 Morrison, "I Imply What You Infer Unless You Are a Court"

1. Implied-in-fact contracts: the *parties* decide that there is a contract. Implied-in-law: the *court* decides.

### 6.4.5 *Day v. Caton*

1. The plaintiff built a wall halfway on his lot and halfway on the defendant's neighboring lot. The plaintiff claimed that the defendant had agreed to pay him for half of the value of the wall, which the defendant denied.

2. The trial court held that the promise might be inferred from the plaintiff's conduct, and the defendant allowed him to finish construction without objection.

3. The court here held for the plaintiff. " . . . when one stands by in silence, and sees valuable services rendered upon his real estate . . . , such silence, accompanied with the knowledge on his part that the party rendering the services expects payment therefor, may fairly be treated as evidence of an acceptance of it, and as tending to show an agreement to pay for it."[286]

---

[282] Casebook p. 505.
[283] Casebook p. 505.
[284] Casebook p. 507.
[285] Casebook p. 508.
[286] Casebook p. 512.

### 6.4.6 Distinguishing Implied-in-Law and Implied-in-Fact: *Bastian v. Gafford*

1. Unjust enrichment is required to show a contract implied in law, but not implied in fact.

### 6.4.7 Remedies for Implied Contracts: *Hill v. Waxberg*

1. Implied-in-fact contracts are based on the parties' intentions, so the proper remedy is compensatory damages.

2. Implied-in-law contracts are based on unjust enrichment, so the proper remedy is the value of the benefit acquired.

### 6.4.8 Unjust Enrichment vs. Quantum Meruit: *Ramsey v. Ellis*

1. Damages in an unjust enrichment (i.e., implied in law) claim are measured by the benefit conferred. Damages in a quantum meruit claim are measured by the reasonable value of the plaintiff's services.

### 6.4.9 Enforceability of Employee Handbooks: *Pine River State Bank v. Mettille*

1. The employer argued that the provisions in its employee handbook because there was no consideration. There was no consideration because employees remained free to go to other employers. The court held that consideration was valid and that mutuality was not required.

### 6.4.10 Modification of Employee Handbooks

1. What happens if the employer modifies the handbook and the employee continues to work? Does the employee's continued work constitute acceptance of the modification? Courts are split.[287]

### 6.4.11 The Effect of Disclaimers in Employee Handbooks

1. Courts are split on whether to enforce disclaimers.[288]

## 6.5 Preliminary Negotiations, Indefiniteness, and the Duty to Bargain in Good Faith

1. Classical contract law drew a strict binary distinction between offer and acceptance, which created a binding agreement, and preliminary negotiations, which did not.[289]

---

[287] Casebook pp. 531–33.
[288] Casebook pp. 533–34.
[289] Casebook p. 536.

2. Agreements can be too indefinite to allow courts to fashion remedies for breach, and are therefore unenforceable.

3. What about agreements to create future agreements? Again classical contract law followed a strict binary: on the one hand, if the future agreement was meant only to confirm the original agreement, the original agreement was enforceable; on the other hand, if the parties intended not to be bound unless they executed the future agreement, the original agreement was not enforceable.

4. Classical contract law recognized no duty to negotiate in good faith.[290]

### 6.5.1 Uncertain and Indefinite: *Academy Chicago Publishers v. Cheever*

1. The Cheevers entered into an agreement with Academy to publish the John Cheever's uncollected stories. The agreement was vague as to the collection's specifications and editorial control.

2. Mrs. Cheever breached the agreement, apparently after realizing the book's potential commercial value.

3. Academy sued to (1) win the exclusive right to publish the collection, (2) designate Franklin Dennis (who was with Mrs. Cheever) as editor, and (3) obligate Mrs. Cheever to deliver the manuscript.

4. The trial court held that the agreement was enforceable, but it granted significant editorial control to Mrs. Cheever. The appellate court affirmed in part and reversed in part.

5. The sole issue before the Supreme Court of Illinois was whether the original agreement was valid and enforceable. It held that "[a]lthough the parties may have had and manifested the intent to make a contract, if the content of their agreement is unduly uncertain and indefinite no contract is formed."[291]

6. The parties lacked a mutual understanding of the essential parts of the agreement. The court cannot substitute the missing terms if they are central to the contract.

7. Reversed.

### 6.5.2 *Ridgway v. Wharton*

1. "An agreement to enter into an agreement upon terms to be afterwards settled between the parties is a contradiction in terms."[292]

---

[290]Casebook p. 537.
[291]Casebook p. 539.
[292]Casebook p. 541.

## 6 ASSENT

### 6.5.3 Berg Agency v. Sleepworld-Willingboro, Inc.

1. If the essential parts of an agreement are included and agreed upon, the contract is enforceable even if other clauses are omitted.[293]

### 6.5.4 Rego v. Decker

1. Courts should fill gaps in contracts where the reasonable expectations of the parties are clear.

2. But, "courts should not impose on a party any performance to which he did not and probably would not have agreed."[294]

### 6.5.5 AROK Construction Co. v. Indian Construction Services

1. Parties may want to create incomplete contracts to allow future flexibility.

### 6.5.6 Saliba-Kringlen Corp. v. Allen Engineering Co.

1. Allen submitted a subcontractor bid to the general contractor, Saliba. Saliba submitted its bid in reliance on Allen's bid.

2. Allen breached, arguing that its bid was too indefinite (and therefore unenforceable) because contained only price and no other details of the contract's performance.

3. The court held for Saliba, finding that there is a general understanding in the trade that subcontractors will enter into an agreement with the general contractor after submitting a winning bid, even if it contained no terms other than the price. If this were not the case, general contractors would be unable to recover § 90 reliance damages.

### 6.5.7 Gap-Fillers

1. The UCC "gap-filler" provisions fill the gaps that parties may leave in contracts for sale of goods.

2. **Default rules**: background rules that the law reads into a contract only if the parties left them out.

3. **Mandatory rules**: not waivable by the parties, e.g., the requirement of consideration.

4. There is controversy over whether the appropriate default rule should be (1) what reasonable people in the parties' positions would have agreed to or (2) what the parties themselves probably would have agreed to given the circumstances. Fuller and Eisenberg favor the first because it avoids

---

[293]Casebook p. 541.
[294]Casebook p. 542.

the complexity of determining the parties' exact position (e.g., bargaining power, degree of risk-averseness).[295]

### 6.5.8 Hawkland, "Sales Contracts Terms under the UCC"

1. Gap-filler terms represent "ordinary understanding" used in "common, unexceptional deals."[296]

### 6.5.9 Agreement to Agree: *Joseph Martin, Jr., Delicatessen, Inc. v. Schumacher*

1. Martin agreed to rent from Schumacher for five years of payments ranging from $500/month to $650/month with the option to renew for another five years "at annual rentals to be agreed upon."[297]

2. Martin tried to renew after the first five-year term. Schumacher demanded $900/month in rent, although the fair market value was less than $550.

3. The trial court held that the agreement was unenforceable for uncertainty. The appellate court reversed, holding that the trial court could set "reasonable rent."

4. The New York Court of Appeals reversed again, holding that there was no method specified in the original agreement about how to calculate rent. As such, the trial court does not have the authority to determine what is reasonable. There was no hint that either party intended to be bound by fair market value.

### 6.5.10 *Moolenaar v. Co-Build Companies, Inc.*

1. Moolenaar agreed to rent land at $350/month, and upon renewal, rent "shall be renegotiated."[298]

2. Co-Build bought the property subject to Moolenaar's lease. At the renewal period, it demanded $17,000/month for the new lease.

3. The court here held that Moolenaar was entitled to "reasonable" rent because (1) it would match the parties' original intent and (2) the parties probably paid valuable consideration for the original agreement, e.g., the landlord benefited by inducing the tenant to pay higher rent on the expectation that the lease would continue.

4. Although this rule is the minority (cf. *Joseph Martin, Jr., Delicatessen* above), the law is moving in this direction.[299]

---

[295]Casebook p. 545.
[296]Casebook p. 545.
[297]Casebook p. 546.
[298]Casebook p. 547.
[299]Casebook pp. 547–48.

*6 ASSENT* 143

### 6.5.11 Good Faith Negotiations: *Channel Home Centers v. Grossman*

Parties can agree to negotiate in good faith.

1. Channel operated a chain of home improvement stores. Grossman owned a mall. The parties began negotiations for leasing to Channel as an anchor tenant in the mall.

2. Channel sent a letter of intent indicating among other things that Grossman would "withdraw the Store from the rental market" during negotiations. Grossman agreed.

3. Soon after, Grossman got a better offer from Mr. Good Buy, one of Channel's competitors. He leased to Mr. Good Buy. Channel sued, claiming that Grossman had violated the letter of intent.

4. The trial court rejected Channel's argument that the letter of intent constituted a binding contract because it did not create any obligation or consideration.

5. On appeal, Channel argued that the letter and the surrounding circumstances created "a binding agreement to negotiate in good faith."[300]

6. The court here held that an agreement to negotiate in good faith is binding if (1) both parties manifested an intention to be bound by the agreement, (2) whether the agreement's terms were definite and therefore enforceable, and (3) whether there was consideration. It held that the agreement between Channel and Grossman met all of these requirements.

7. Held, Grossman violated its obligation to negotiate in good faith.

## 6.6 The Parol Evidence Rule and the Interpretation of Written Contracts

### 6.6.1 The Parol Evidence Rule

#### 6.6.1.1 Thayer, "A Preliminary Treatise on Evidence"

1. Some want a "lawyer's Paradise" where written instruments have a precise, fixed meaning. But in reality, context is a "fatal necessity."[301]

---
[300] Casebook p. 553.
[301] Casebook p. 590.

### 6.6.1.2 Calamari & Perillo, "A Plea for a Uniform Parol Evidence Rule and Principles of Interpretation"

1. There is basic disagreement about the meaning of the parol evidence rule and of the goals of contractual interpretation.

2. There is substantial agreement that later final expressions replace earlier tentative expressions.

3. Disagreement arises when the last expression is not in writing. Imagine A sells property to B on the condition, agreed orally, that A will remove an unsightly shack from neighboring property. Can the oral promise be enforced?

4. The answer depends on whether the written agreement was a **total integration**.[302]

    (a) *Williston*: the existence of the oral agreement proves that the written agreement was only a partial intergration. The only question would be whether the parties actually made the alleged prior oral agreement. A written expression is presumptively a complete integration unless it would be natural for similarly situated parties to add additional terms in a separate (oral) agreement.[303]

    (b) *Corbin*: Williston's approach—excluding relevant evidence of intent except the writing itself—is absurd.

5. The core of the debate is whether it is better to allow oral evidence or to require the parties to put their entire agreement in formal, written terms.[304]

### 6.6.1.3 Restatement First §§ 228, 237, 239, 240

1. § 228: an integrated agreement is final and complete.

2. § 237: an integrated agreement nullifies all previous agreements and all contemporaneous oral agreements.

3. § 239: effect of partial integration.

4. § 240: Integration does not supersede earlier agreements if it is consistent and (1) made for separate consideration or (2) would naturally be separate.

---

[302] Casebook p. 592.
[303] Casebook pp. 591–92.
[304] Casebook p. 592.

## 6 ASSENT

### 6.6.1.4 Braucher, "Interpretation and Legal Effect in the Second Restatement of Contracts"

1. The difficulties in parol evidence lie in:[305]

    (a) Determining whether there is an integrated agreement.

    (b) Whether the agreement is completely or partially integrated.

    (c) Whether the prior agreement is consistent with and within the scope of the integrated agreement.

### 6.6.1.5 *Hatley v. Stafford*

1. In determining whether oral terms would have naturally been included in the written agreement, courts should look to contextual factors beyond the face of the document, including the parties' business experience, whether they are represented by counsel, their relative bargaining power, and the completeness and detail of the writing itself.[306]

2. Courts should presume complete integration, "and should admit evidence of consistent additional terms only if there is substantial evidence that the parties did not intend the writing to embody the entire agreement."[307]

### 6.6.1.6 *Interform Co. v. Mitchell Constr. Co.*

1. The debate between Corbin and Williston centers on "the attitude with which judges should approach written contracts."[308]

2. Williston: the judge should ascertain the legal relations between the parties through form—i.e., the parties' use of normal integration practices and language. The contract means what a reasonably intelligent person would understand them to mean.

3. Corbin: the judge should ascertain the legal relations between the parties on the basis of the parties' intent, regardless of their use of forms. The contract means what the parties intended it to mean.

4. Corbin's influence is stronger.[309]

### 6.6.1.7 Murray, "The Parol Evidence Process and Standardized Agreements under the Restatement, Second, Contracts"

1. The Restatement Second's rule in § 209 determines whether an agreement is integrated as "a question of fact to be determined in accordance with all relevant evidence." The Restatement follows Corbin, who argued "no relevant testimony should be excluded."[310]

---

[305] Casebook p. 593.
[306] Casebook p. 593.
[307] Casebook p. 594.
[308] Casebook p. 594.
[309] Casebook p. 594.
[310] Casebook p. 595.

# 6 ASSENT

### 6.6.1.8 Dodge, "Teaching the CISG in Contracts"

1. "... the CISG lacks a parol evidence rule and allows a court interpreting a written contract to consider not just trade usage, course of dealing, and course of performance, but even parties' prior negotiations."[311]

### 6.6.1.9 *Masterson v. Sine*

1. The Mastersons conveyed a ranch to the Sines. Medora Sine was Dallas Masterson's sister. The conveyance gave the Mastersons a purchase option for the following ten years for the "same consideration as being paid heretofore plus their depreciation value of any improvements Grantees may add to the property from and after two and a half years from this date."[312]

2. Dallas Masterson went bankrupt. His trustee and his wife, Rebecca, brought suit to establish their right to enforce the option.

3. The trial court held that the Mastersons could exercise their option.

4. On appeal, the dispute centered on whether the trial court properly excluded evidence that "that the option was personal to the grantors and therefore nonassignable."[313]

5. When an agreement is only partially integrated, parol evidence can "prove elements of the agreement not reduced to writing."[314]

6. The option clause in the deed did not provide that it contained the complete agreement.

7. In this case, the alleged additional terms (that the option was personal and nonassignable) might reasonably have left it out of the written deed.

8. Therefore, the trial court erred in excluding parol evidence of the parties' agreement that the option was not assignable.

### 6.6.1.10 *Interform v. Mitchell Constr. Co.*

1. UCC § 2-202 reflects Corbin's influence in its focus on the intent of the parties, rather than the practices of reasonable people.

---

[311] Casebook p. 595.
[312] Casebook p. 595.
[313] Casebook p. 596.
[314] Casebook p. 596.

## 6 ASSENT

### 6.6.1.11 *Hunt Foods and Industries, Inc. v. Doliner*

1. Hunt began negotiations to buy Eastern Can Company. Doliner owned the majority of Eastern's stock. It became necessary to pause the negotiations. Doliner granted Hunt an option to purchase Doliner's stock at $5.50/share. Doliner alleged that there was an additional oral agreement that the option "was only to be used in the event that he solicited an outside offer."[315]

2. Negotiations fell through. Hunt exercised its option. Doliner refused to deliver the stock, so Hunt sued, requesting summary judgment.

3. Hunt argued that the alleged condition could not be proved under the parol evidence rule.

4. UCC § 2-202 provides that parol evidence may explain or supplement a written agreement agreement, but not contradict it. According to the court, a term is inconsistent if it contradicts or negates a term of the writing. If it does not, it is admissible.

5. In this case, the alleged modification—that Hunt could exercise the option only if Doliner got another offer—was consistent with the written agreement and therefore admissible.

6.

### 6.6.1.12 *Alaska Northern Development, Inc. v. Alyeska Pipeline Service Co.*

1. The *Hunt Foods* view of consistency is too narrow. A better definition is "the absence of reasonable harmony in terms of the language and respective obligations of the parties."[316]

### 6.6.1.13 Merger Clauses

1. Merger (or integration) clauses provide that the written contract is the entire agreement between the parties.[317]

2. Often, a merger clause is not enough to prove complete integration. Courts often hold that the parties must have actually assented to integration.

### 6.6.1.14 *ARB (American Research Bureau), Inc. v. E-Systems, Inc.*

1. Courts must consider surrounding circumstances to determine whether the parties actually assented to the merger clause.

---

[315] Casebook p. 600.
[316] Casebook p. 601.
[317] Casebook p. 602.

### 6.6.1.15 Siebel v. Layne & Bowler, Inc.

1. UCC § 2-202 requires intent to integrate in addition to a merger clause. In a written contract, the merger clause must be conspicuous.

### 6.6.1.16 The Fraud Exception to the Parol Evidence Rule

1. Otherwise inadmissible parol evidence is admissible if it shows an "invalidating cause" of the written agreement—e.g., lack of consideration, duress, mistake, illegality, or fraud.[318]

### 6.6.1.17 The Condition-to-Legal Effectiveness Exception to the Parol Evidence Rule

1. The parol evidence rule does not apply when the occurrence or nonoccurence of an event, by spoken agreement, is a condition to making the written agreement binding or effective.[319]

2. For instance, A and B make a written business agreement, and agree orally that the agreement will be null if the parties fail to raise $600,000 within 20 days. Evidence of the oral agreement is admissible.

3. Two criticisms:

    (a) If the parol agreement is a condition to *performance* of a written agreement, the parol agreement is inadmissible because the written agreement is a binding contract. But if the parol agreement is a condition to the *legal effectiveness* of the written agreement, the parol agreement is admissible.

    (b) This exception is hard to reconcile with the parol evidence rule. The rational for the condition-to-legal effectiveness rule is that if a parol agreement indicated that a written agreement would not be effective until an additional condition was met, then the written instrument is not a contract, so the parol evidence rule does not apply. The difficulty is that in most cases where the exception applies, the written agreement *is* a contract, and the parol agreement was a condition to the obligation of performance, rather than a condition to the contract's legal effectiveness. In the above example, for instance, A would likely be in breach of contract for failing to raise the $600,000.

### 6.6.1.18 No Oral Modification Clauses

1. The parol evidence rule applies only to oral agreements made before or contemporaneously with a written, integrated contract. The rule **doesn't apply to a later agreement that modifies the integration**.[320]

---
[318] Casebook p. 604.
[319] Casebook p. 606.
[320] Casebook p. 208.

# 6 ASSENT

2. However, the later oral agreement may be invalid under the legal duty rule or the Statute of Frauds.

3. Written contracts often provide that they can be modified only in writing—a private Statute of Frauds. These are **no oral modification (n.o.m.)** clauses.

4. Common law: oral modifications are enforceable notwithstanding n.o.m. clauses, because the later oral agreement by implication modifies the earlier written agreement containing the n.o.m. clause.

5. Example: "I'll pay ypu $100 to lock me in this room. Don't let me out for 10 hours, no matter what I say." You sign the agreement. At common law, cries of "I changed my mind, I'll pay you $500 to let me out!" would modify the original agreement.

6. UCC § 2-209 makes two key changes to the common law:

    (a) § 2-209(1): a modification needs no consideration to be enforceable.

    (b) § 2-209(2): if a contract for the sale of goods contains a n.o.m. clause, the modification must be in writing.

7. But, § 2-209(4) allows that an attempt at modification under § 2-209(2) can operate as a waiver. But then § 2-209(5) provides that a party who has created a waiver for an executory (unperformed) part of the contract can retract it if the other party has relied on the waiver.

### 6.6.2 The Interpretation of Written Contracts

#### 6.6.2.1 Plain Meaning: *Steuart v. McChesney*

1. The Steuarts granted a right of first refusal on a piece of farmland to the McChesneys. It provided that if the Steuarts got a bone fide offer for the land, the McChesneys could buy it for the market value as assessed for the county and state real estate tax levy.

2. Later, the Steuarts got offers for $30,000 and $35,000. A commercial appraiser valued it at $50,000. But the government appraisal valued it at $7,820.

3. The McChesneys sued for specific performance.

4. "... where language is clear and unambiguous, the focus of interpretation is upon the terms of the agreement as *manifestly* expressed, rather than as, perhaps, silently intended."[321]

5. Despite controversy over the plain meaning rule, the court here decided to follow it.

---

[321] Casebook p. 608.

# 6 ASSENT

6. The trial court held that the government value was a "protective minimum" rather than a "controlling price."[322]

7. The appellate court reversed, following the agreement's plain meaning. The court here affirmed.

8. Justice Roberts, dissenting: the government's assessment was outdated. It's not fair to make the parties adhere to it.

### 6.6.2.2 Mellon Bank, N.A. v. Aetna Business Credit, Inc.

1. The judge's linguistic reference point is necessarily different than the parties'. Parties should be allowed to introduce reasonable alternative interpretations of the written agreement.

### 6.6.2.3 Amoco Production Co. v. Western Slope Gas Co.

1. UCC § 2-202 assumes that the written contract is not completely integrated. Under the UCC, the court should admit parole evidence by default unless the judge thinks the written agreement is unambiguous.

### 6.6.2.4 Pacific Gas & Electric Co. v. G.W. Thomas Drayage & Rigging Co.

1. PG&E contracted with Thomas Drayage to repair a steam turbine. The contract included an indemnity clause providing that Drayage would indemnify PG&E "against all loss, damage, expense and liability resulting from . . . injury to property . . ."[323]

2. The turbine was damaged during the work. PG&E sued to recover the $25,144.51 it spent on repairs. The trial court held for PG&E "on the theory that the indemnity provision covered injury to all property regardless of ownership."[324]

3. Drayage wanted to introduce parol evidence showing that the parties meant for the indemnity clause to apply only to damage to property of third parties, not to PG&E's property. But the trial court held that the contract had a plain meaning, so it excluded the parol evidence.

4. But language lacks fixed meaning. "Accordingly, rational interpretation requires at least a preliminary consideration of all credible evidence offered to prove the intention of the parties."[325]

---
[322]Casebook p. 609.
[323]Casebook p. 615.
[324]Casebook p. 615.
[325]Casebook p. 617.

### 6.6.2.5 *Garden State Plaza Corp. v. S.S. Kresge Co.*

1. The parol evidence rule does not come into play until the court determines the meaning of the written agreement. In interpreting and constructing the written agreement, courts must allow all relevant evidence indicating its meaning, including evidence from the circumstances of the creation of the agreement.

2. But, external evidence is invalid if it gives the agreement "a meaning completely alien to anything its words can possibly express."[326]

### 6.6.2.6 *Trident Center v. Connecticut General Life Ins. Co.*

1. Trident obtained financing for a construction project from Connecticut General. The contract provided for a $56.5 million loan at 12.25% interest for 15 years, without the ability to prepay the principal for the first 12 years. If it defaulted before year 12, Trident could accelerate payment and add a 10% prepayment fee.

2. Five years later, interest rates dropped. Trident sued for a declaration saying that it could prepay the loan, subject only to the 10% prepayment fee. Connecticut General argued that the contract unambiguously precluded prepayment before 12 years. The district court granted Trident's motion to dismiss.

3. The Ninth Circuit reversed. Judge Kozinksi:

    (a) The language is unambiguous, but nonetheless Trident interpreted it as granting the right to prepay.

    (b) Trident was seeking "judicial sterilization of its intended default."[327]

    (c) In the alternative, Trident sought to introduce external evidence showing that the actual agreement was quite different.

    (d) The court grudgingly agreed that the external evidence must be allowed under the California Supreme Court's holding in *Pacific Gas*—which "we have no difficulty understanding ..., even without extrinsic evidence to guide us."[328]

---

[326] Casebook p. 618.
[327] Casebook p. 620.
[328] Casebook p. 621.

# § 7 Form Contracts

## 7.1 Contract Formation in a Form-Contract Setting

### 7.1.1 Battle of the Forms: The Basic Issues

1. **Battle of the forms**: buyers and sellers exchange elaborate preprinted form contracts. It would be prohibitively costly for buyers to actually read the boilerplate terms (**rational ignorance**).[329]

2. The **last shot** rule: under classical contract law, conduct can constitute acceptance—e.g., the buyer could tacitly accept the terms of the deal by accepting and keeping the goods. In that case, the last form the parties exchanges would control.[330]

3. UCC § 2-204: general formation of a contract.

4. UCC § 2-207: there can be a contract even if the language of the forms differs. The conflicting language is removed and, if necessary, replaced with gap-fillers. It rejects the mirror image rule.

   (a) The premise behind § 2-207 is that no rational person reads the boilerplate terms.

#### 7.1.1.1 What constitutes acceptance under UCC § 2-207?

1. Courts have held that there is an "expression of acceptance" when forms are involved and only the individualized terms match, but none of the boilerplate terms match. But if forms aren't involved, slight differences between offer and acceptance will invalidate the contract if the parties have been bargaining about that term.[331]

#### 7.1.1.2 *Columbia Hyundai, Inc. v. Carll Hyundai, Inc.*

1. Gibbes negotiated to buy Carll's Hyundai dealership. Gibbes signed a written agreement but added the phrase "current year" before "vehicles."

2. The court held that there had been no contract. § 2-207 did not apply because this was a non-form, fully negotiated agreement. "Under such circumstances, when the parties fully negotiate each provision of a contract, a contract may be 'beyond the reach of 2-207 and adrift on the murky sea of common law.'"[332]

---

[329] Casebook pp. 639–40.
[330] Casebook pp. 641–42.
[331] Casebook p. 643.
[332] Casebook p. 644.

# 7 FORM CONTRACTS

### 7.1.1.3 "Expressly Conditional": *Gardner Zemke Co. v. Dunham Bush, Inc.*

1. Gardner sent a purchase order for air conditioners to Dunham. Dunham's acknowledgment contained different terms.

2. After a dispute over repair obligations, Gardner argued that the Dunham's customer agreement was a counteroffer. Dunham argued that it was.

3. responding document will fall outside 2-207, and act as a counteroffer, if "acceptance is expressly made conditional on assent to the additional or different terms." Dunham argued that its acknowledgment contained provisions that made acceptance conditional on assent to additional terms, and was therefore a counteroffer.

4. The court here held that it's not enough to make acceptance expressly conditional on additional terms. Rather, the "the expressly conditional nature of the acceptance must be predicated on the offeror's 'assent' to those terms." In other words, if the dickered terms are identical but the undickered terms vary, the transaction does not become "expressly conditional" and the response does not become a counteroffer.

### 7.1.1.4 The Meaning of "Materially Alter" under UCC § 2-207(2)(b)

1. A term added in an acceptance does not become part of the contract if it would "materially alter" the contract. The UCC defines "materially alter" to mean "would result in [unreasonable] surprise or hardship." So, for instance, a mandatory arbitration clause is not a material alteration.[333]

### 7.1.1.5 The "Expressly Made Conditional" Clause in UCC § 2-207

1. Courts are split. Some hold that that if acceptance is "expressly made conditional," it must be "directly and distinctly stated."[334] Others apply looser standards, e.g., requiring certain key phrases, or requiring the offeree to demonstrate unwillingness to proceed unless he agrees to the additional terms.

## 7.2 "Rolling Contracts"

### 7.2.1 Shrinkwrap Agreements: *ProCD, Inc. v. Zeidenberg*

1. ProCD sold consumer information databases on CDs. It sold at a higher price to commercial users. It used a license, encoded on the CDs and printed in the user manual, to enforce its price discrimination system. The user was required to agree to the license agreement each time the application ran.

---

[333]Casebook pp. 653–55.
[334]Casebook p. 655.

# 7 FORM CONTRACTS

2. Zeidenberg published ProCD's databases online. ProCD sued for an injunction on the ground that Zeidenberg had violated the license agreement.

3. The district court held that the licenses were ineffectual because their terms did not appear on the outside of the packages.

4. Zeidenberg that he was only bound by terms that were printed on the outside of the box.

5. The Seventh Circuit here held that there are plenty of examples of "[t]ransactions in which the exchange of money precedes the communication of detailed terms"—e.g., insurance, airline tickets, consumer electronics, or software bought online. The customer can assent to the additional terms by using the product, or he can reject the terms by using the product.

6. The UCC permits this type of **"money now, terms later"** agreement.

7. "In the end, the terms of the license are conceptually identical to the contents of the package."[335]

8. Reversed.

## 7.2.2 Applying *ProCD* to Hardware: *Hill v. Gateway 2000*

1. The Hills bought a Gateway PC. Inside the box was an agreement which included an arbitration clause. The agreement indicated that it was binding if the customer did not return the computer within 30 days. The Hills kept the computer for more than 30 days.

2. The Hills sued to invalidate the arbitration clause. The district court refused to enforce the clause.

3. There was no reason to limit *ProCD* to software. For instance, why require a salesperson to read an entire four-page document over the phone to a customer?

4. The Hills argued that *ProCD* should only apply to executory contracts, and did not apply in this case because performance was complete when the Hills opened the box. The court held that this argument was wrong legally because the issue is contract formation, not performance, and wrong factually because both contracts were incompletely performed (e.g., the Hills invoked Gateway's warranty, which was available to them only after they opened the box and read the additional terms).

5. It didn't matter whether there were terms on the outside of the Gateway box.

6. The agreement, including the arbitration clause, was enforceable.

---
[335]Casebook p. 669.

## 7 FORM CONTRACTS

### 7.2.3 Clickwrap Agreements: *Specht v. Netscape Communications Corp.*

Clickwrap agreements require "[r]easonably conspicuous notice of the existence of contract terms and unambiguous manifestation of assent to those terms by consumers . . ."[336]

1. Plaintiffs in three related class actions downloaded Netscape SmartDownload. They alleged that SmartDownload contained code to allow Netscape to eavesdrop on their downloading activity.

2. Users who downloaded SmartDownload did not have to agree to a clickwrap agreement to download or install the software. The license terms were on the download page, but the use would have had to scroll down to find them.

3. One of the terms in the SmartDownload license agreement was an arbitration clause.

4. In district court, Netscape moved to compel arbitration. The court held that the page did not alert users to the license agreement nor require their assent.

5. Judge Sotomayor (Second Circuit):

    (a) Offerees are not bound by inconspicuous terms of which he is unaware in a document that is not obviously a contract.[337]

    (b) "Inquiry notice": circumstances to put a reasonable person on actual notice. Netscape argued that users were on inquiry notice of the license agreement. But the court held that the terms were not apparent to the user nor obviously contractual.

    (c) "We conclude that in circumstances such as these, where consumers are urged to download free software at the immediate click of a button, a reference to the existence of license terms on a submerged screen is not sufficient to place consumers on inquiry or constructive notice of those terms."[338]

    (d) Affirmed.

## 7.3 Interpretation and Unconscionability in a Form Contract Setting

### 7.3.1 Reformation and Mutual Mistake: *Sardo v. Fidelity & Deposit Co.*

1. Sardo bought insurance to insure the jewelry in his store against theft. Fidelity issued a policy covering "money and securities." Sardo assumed

---
[336] Casebook p. 686.
[337] Casebook p. 682.
[338] Casebook p. 684.

## 7 FORM CONTRACTS

that "securities" included jewelry, but the contract included a specific definition of "securities" that clearly did not include jewelry.

2. Sardo's store was robbed. Sardo sued to force Fidelity to reimburse him for the lost jewelry.

3. The trial court held that the contract should be reformed to change "securities" to "jewelry."[339]

4. The appellate court here reversed, holding that reformation is appropriate only in the case of mutual mistake. But here, only Sardo made a mistake.

### 7.3.2 Llewellyn, "The Common Law Tradition: Deciding Appeals"

1. Form contracts are attractive. But they can take on "a massive and almost terrifying jug-handled character."[340] Nobody really reads them.

2. So, nobody really assents to boilerplate terms. Rather, people only really assent to the dickered terms.

3. "[A]ny contract with boiler-plate results in *two* several contracts: the *dickered* deal, and the collateral one of *supplementary* boiler-plate."[341]

### 7.3.3 *Weaver v. American Oil Co.*

1. American Oil leased a gas station to Weaver each year. The lease included a clause that exculpated American Oil from liability for its negligence and compelled Weaver to indemnify them for damages resulting from its negligence.

2. Weaver hadn't finished high school. He never read the lease and nobody explained its terms to him. He lacked any awareness of the indemnity clause.

3. If the contract had been for the sale of goods, it would have been unconscionable under UCC § 2-302.[342]

4. The clause was buried in the contract.

5. The parties' actual understanding of the agreement should outweigh the parol evidence rule. This agreement "should not be enforceable on the grounds that the provision is contrary to public policy."[343]

6. Indemnity clauses are fine if the parties agree to them knowingly and willingly.

---

[339]Casebook p. 693.
[340]Casebook p. 694.
[341]Casebook p. 696.
[342]Casebook p. 697.
[343]Casebook p. 699.

## § 8 Mistake and Unexpected Circumstances

### 8.1 Mistake

#### 8.1.1 Unilateral Mistakes (Mechanical Errors)

#### 8.1.1.1 The Nolan Ryan Baseball Card Case

1. Bryan Wrzesinski bought a baseball card worth $1,200 for $12. The cashier apparently didn't know its worth. The owner of the store sued to recover either the card or damages.[344]

2. The parties settled, auctioning of the card and giving the proceeds to charity.

3. The facts are ambiguous, but under any scenario, Bryan either misled the cashier or knew that the price tag was the result of a mechanical error.

#### 8.1.1.2 Unilateral Mistake

1. " . . . relief will not be granted unless the other party has either not relied *or* cannot be restored to his precontractual position by the award of reliance damages."[345]

#### 8.1.2 Mistakes in Transcription; Reformation

#### 8.1.2.1 *Travelers Ins. Co. v. Bailey*

1. Bailey bought life insurance. The plan he applied for was for $5,000 plus a retirement annuity for $500 per *year*.

2. His policy documents said that the annuity was $500 per *month*.

3. Bailey brought the issue to Travelers' attention, and it issued a new policy.

4. "Where, as here, an antecedent contract has been established by the requisite measure of proof, equity will act to bring the erroneous writing into conformity with the true agreement."[346] Unilateral mistakes call for reformation.

5. " . . . we hold that where there has been established beyond a reasonable doubt a specific contractual agreement between parties, and a aubsequent erroneous rendition of the terms of the agreement in a material particular, the party penalized by the error is entitled to reformation, if there has been no prejudicial change of position by the other party while ignorant of the mistake."[347]

---

[344]Casebook p. 727.
[345]Casebook p. 728.
[346]Casebook pp. 729–30.
[347]Casebook pp. 730–31.

# 8 MISTAKE AND UNEXPECTED CIRCUMSTANCES

### 8.1.2.2 *Chimart Associates v. Paul*

1. "... reformation based upon mistake is not available where the parties purposely contract based upon uncertain or contingent events."[348]

2. The party claiming mistake or fraud must prove it with certainty, and must also prove what the parties actually agreed to.

## 8.1.3 Mutual Mistakes (Shared Mistaken Assumptions)

1. **Shared mistaken assumptions**: tacit or explicit assumptions in the agreement turn out to be incorrect.

2. Tacit assumptions are always present (e.g., the sun will rise tomorrow). No agreement could possibly render all of them explicit.

### 8.1.3.1 Barren Cow: *Sherwood v. Walker*

1. "Replevin for a cow."[349]

2. Sherwood contracted to buy a cow from Walker. Everyone thought the cow was probably barren, so he bought it for only $80.

3. After agreeing to sell it, the defendants realized the cow was pregnant, so they refused to give it to Sherwood. Sherwood sued for performance.

4. The trial court held for Sherwood. The appellate court ("circuit court of Wayne county") affirmed.[350]

5. The circuit judge instructed the jury that if it found that the defendants intended to transfer title to the cow when they confirmed Sherwood's order, the agreement was valid. It didn't matter when or where the cow was held.[351]

6. The defendants argued that title did not pass until the cow was weighed and the price determined (because the price was based on weight), and that "the barrenness of the cow was a condition precedent to pasing title..."[352]

7. Here, the court held that a party can refuse to perform a contract "if the assent was founded, or the contract made, upon the mistake of a material fact..."[353]

---

[348]Casebook p. 731.
[349]Casebook p. 733.
[350]Casebook p. 733.
[351]Casebook p. 735.
[352]Casebook p. 736.
[353]Casebook p. 736.

8. "The difficulty in every case is to determine whether the mistake or misapprehension is as to the **substance** of the whole contract, going, as it were, to the root of the matter, or only to **some point**, even though a material point, an error as to which does not affect the substance of the whole consideration."[354]

9. The mistake as to the cow's barrenness "went to the **whole substance** of the agreement."[355] "She was sold as a beef creature would be sold; she is in fact a breeding cow, and a valuable one."[356]

10. Held: if the jury determines that the cow was fertile, the court should allow the defendants to rescind the contract.

11. Judge Sherwood, dissenting:

    (a) The plaintiff thought the cow would breed. He entered the agreement on the basis of his judgment.

    (b) " . . . it is held that because it turned out that the plaintiff was more correct in his judgment as to one quality of the cow than the defendants, and a quality, too, which could not by any possibility be positively known at the time by either party to exist, the contract may be annulled by the defendants at their pleasure."[357]

    (c) "When a mistaken fact is relied upon as ground for rescinding, such fact must not only exist at the time the contract is made, but must have been known to one or both of the parties."[358]

    (d) Here, neither party knew whether the cow was barren. The defendants shouldn't be able to rescind because they misjudged the cow's fertility.

### 8.1.3.2  Nester v. Michigan Land & Iron Co.

1. Michigan Land sold "all the merchantable pine" on a lot to Nester. The agreement required Nester to estimate the amound of timber on the land.

2. After purchasing the rights, Nester discovered that the quality and amount of timber were far below what he expected. He sued to reduce the purchase price by 50%.

3. The court held for Michigan Land. Judge Sherwood, who dissented a year earlier in *Sherwood*, wrote the opinion, holding that the *Sherwood* rule applies only when "all the facts and circumstances are precisely the same as in that."[359]

---

[354]Casebook p. 736.
[355]Casebook p. 736.
[356]Casebook p. 737.
[357]Casebook p. 738.
[358]Casebook p. 738.
[359]Casebook p. 739.

### 8.1.3.3 Griffith v. Brymer

1. Griffith paid Brymer £100 to rent a room to watch the Coronation Procession.

2. That morning, the King decided to undergo surgery and cancelled the procession, unbeknownst to Griffith and Brymer.

3. Griffith sued to recover the money.

4. The court held that the agreement was based on a supposition that made performance impossible, "which went to the whole root of the matter."[360] Griffith could recover his £100.

### 8.1.3.4 Wood v. Boynton

1. Wood brought a small stone to Boynton, a jeweler. He offered her $1 for it. She declined. Later, she needed money, so she returned to Boynton and accepted his offer. It turned out to be an uncut diamond, though neither of them knew it. Wood sued for rescission.

2. Held for Boynton: "However unfortunate the plaintiff may have been in selling this valuable stone for a mere nominal sum, she has failed entirely to make out a case either of fraud or mistake in the sale such as will entitle her to a rescission . . ."[361]

3. Was there a mistake in this case? The court says no.

### 8.1.3.5 Firestone & Parson, Inc. v. Union League of Philadelphia

1. Union League owned a painting called "The Bombardment of Fort Sumter," generally regarded as a major work of Albert Bierstadt.

2. Firestone bought the painting from Union League in 1981 for $500,000.

3. By 1986, art critics agreed that the painting was the work of another artist, John Ross Key.

4. In 1988 Firestone sued for rescission, arguing that as a Bierstadt the painting was worth more than $500,000, but as a Key it was worth only $50,000.

5. The court held that there had not been a mistake. "Post-sale fluctuations in generally accepted attributions do not necessarily establish that there was a mutural mistake of fact at the time of the sale."[362] Since art critics generally agreed in 1981 that the painting was a Bierstadt, then there was no mutual mistake of fact.

---

[360] Casebook p. 740.
[361] Casebook p. 741.
[362] Casebook p. 743.

### 8.1.3.6 Everett v. Estate of Sumstad

1. The Mitchells bought a $50 safe at an auction. The inner compartment was locked and the key had been lost, so they hired a locksmith to open it. Inside was $32,207.

2. " . . . we hold reasonable persons would conclude that the auctioneer manifested an objective intent to sell the safe and its contents and that the parties mutually assented to enter into that sale of the safe and the contents of the locked compartment."[363]

### 8.1.3.7 "Basic Assumption": *Lenawee County Board of Health v. Messerly*

1. In 1971, Bloom conveyed one acre plus six hundred square feet to the Messerlys. There was a three-unit apartment building on the 600 square foot portion. Bloom had improperly installed a septic tank.

2. In 1973, the Messerlys sold it on a land contract to Barnes. The Barnses defaulted, so in 1977, the Messerlys executed a land contract with the Pickleses. It included as-is and integration clauses.[364]

3. Fix or six days later, the Pickleses noticed raw sewage seeping out of the ground. The Lewanee County Board of Health condemned the property and brought suit against the Messerlys and Pickleses to win a permanent injunction prohibiting human habitation until the property conformed with the sanitation code.

4. The Pickleses made no payment on the contract. The Messerlys cross-claimed against the Pickleses, seeking foreclosure, sale, and a deficiency judgment. The Pickleses counterclaimed for rescission and filed a third-party complaint against the Barneses. The Pickleses alleged failure of consideration and misrepresentation.

5. The trial court held that the Pickleses had no cause of action against either the Barnses or the Messerlys because there was no fraud or misrepresentation. Nobody knew of Bloom's "transgression" until the Pickleses discovered the sewage leak. The as-is clause protected the seller. The court granted foreclosure and damages in the amount of the land contract ($25,943.09).

6. The appellate court affirmed as to the Barnses but reversed as to the Messerlys, holding that "the mutual mistake . . . went to a basic, as opposed to a collateral, element of the contract, and that the parties intended to transfer income-producing rental property but, in actuality, the vendees paid $25,500 for an asset without value."[365]

---

[363]Casebook p. 743.
[364]Casebook p. 744.
[365]Casebook p. 745.

7. A contractual mistake "must relate to a fact in existence at the time the contract is executed."[366]

8. The septic system was defective before the Pickleses executed their agreement. Therefore, there was a mutual mistake.

9. The Barnses and Messerlys argued that the mistake was collateral to the agreement. The Pickleses argued that it was "pervasive and essential," citing *Sherwood*.[367]

10. The court here rejected the *Sherwood* rule, limiting it to the facts in that case. It replaced it with the **basic assumption rule**: " . . . rescission is indicated when the mistaken belief relates to a basic assumption of the parties upon which the contract is made, and which materially affects the agreed performance of the party."[368]

11. However, even in such cases, courts need not grant rescission. "Equity suggests that, in this case, the risk should be allocated to the purchases."[369] The as-is clause allocated the risk to the Pickleses. The Pickleses were not entitled to rescission. Reversed.

### 8.1.3.8 *Beachcomber Coins, Inc. v. Boskett*

1. Beachcomber bought a coin for $500 from Boskett. It was purportedly a dime minted in Denver in 1916. Beachcomber later learned that it was a counterfeit. He sued for rescission based on mutual mistake.

2. The trial judge held for Boskett on the ground that a dealer has an obligation to determine the genuineness of the coin, and he assumes the risk when he makes the purchase.

3. The appellate court here reversed. "[N]egligent failure of a party to know or to discover the facts as to which both parties are under a mistake does not preclude rescission or reformation on account thereof."[370]

4. The buyer's assumption of risk is relevant only when the parties are aware of the possibility that they were wrong. Here, both parties were certain that the coin was genuine. It would've been different if the buyer was uncertain about the coin's genuineness and accepted the buyer's expert judgment.

## 8.2 The Effect of Unexpected Circumstances

1. Impossibility, impracticability, frustration.

---

[366] Casebook p. 745.
[367] Casebook p. 746.
[368] Casebook p. 747.
[369] Casebook p. 748.
[370] Casebook p. 749.

## 8.2.1 Implied Condition: *Taylor v. Caldwell*

1. The plaintiffs contracted with the defendants to rent The Surrey Gardens and Music Hall for four nights. The hall burned down before the specified nights. The plaintiff sued to recover payment and other losses.

2. The existence of the hall was an **implied condition**.[371]

3. " . . . in contracts in which the performance depends on the continued existence of a given person or thing, a condition is implied that the possibility of performance arising from the perishing or the person or thing shall excuse the performance."[372]

## 8.2.2 Tacit Assumptions—Continued

1. Contracts involve many tacit assumptions.

2. "We 'just know' that the burning of a music hall violates a tacit assumption of the parties who executed a contract for hiring it for a few days; we 'just know' that a two per cent increase in the price of beans does not violate a tacit assumption underlying a contract to deliver a ton of beans for a fixed price."[373]

## 8.2.3 *Ocean Tramp Tankers Corp. v. V/O Sovfracht*

1. The theory of an implied term suggests that if an implied term is violated, the deal is off. *Taylor v. Caldwell*. But the parties likely wouldn't want to just end the deal. They would probably want to modify it instead.

## 8.2.4 Impracticality: *Mineral Park Land Co. v. Howard*

1. The defendants were building a bridge across a ravine, which the plaintiffs owned. They agreed that the defendants would take all necessary gravel and earth for the project from the plaintiffs' land.

2. The defendants took 50,869 cubic yards from the plaintiffs' land, but used 101,000 total in the project.

3. Plaintiff sued for breach. The court held for the defendants because, although the plaintiffs' land contained more than enough earth and gravel, only 50,131 cubic yards were above water and accessible. The rest of the gravel and earth on the plaintiffs' land was impractical (and thus "impossible in legal contemplation") to retrieve.[374]

---

[371] Casebook p. 766.
[372] Casebook p. 768.
[373] Casebook p. 769.
[374] Casebook p. 770.

### 8.2.5 Bad Gamble: *United States v. Wegematic Corp.*

1. Wegematic secured a contract to sell a computer to the Federal Reserve Board. It had difficulty finishing the order on time, so it ultimately requested cancellation.

2. The Board bought and IBM machine instead and sued Wegematic for damages.

3. Wegematic argued that delivery was impossible because of "basic engineering difficulties," which it argued constituted a "practical impossibility."[375]

4. UCC § 2-615 governs practical impossibility.

5. The court held that Wegematic gambled that it could develop the technology and ship the order within the agreed time. It lost. If Wegematic were allowed to raise impossibility as a defense, technology manufacturers "would thus enjoy a wide degree of latitude with respect to performance while holding an option to compel the buyer to pay if the gamble should pan out."[376]

### 8.2.6 Commercial Impracticability: *Missouri Public Service Co. v. Peabody Coal Co.*

1. Peabody agreed to supply coal to Public Service at $5.40 per ton. The agreement included an escalation clause that would increase the price per ton according to the Industrial Commodities Index.

2. The price of coal rose. Peabody tried to negotiate a new price, but Public Service would only add $1.00 per ton. Peabody notified Public Service of its intent to breach, so Public Service sued.

3. Among other defenses, Peabody argued that UCC § 2-615 offered a defense of commercial impracticability on the basis of excuse by failure of presupposed conditions. Specifically, Peabody argued (1) that the Industrial Commodities Index was no longer an accurate measure of inflation, and (2) the oil embargo had driven up prices.

4. The court here held that Peabody was aware of the behavior of the Industrial Commodities Index, so it foresaw or should have foreseen the Index's divergence from other measures. The court also held that Peabody failed to show that the embargo caused financial hardship.

5. Peabody made a bad bargain, but "this fact alone does not deal with either the 'basic assumption' on which the contract was negotiated or alter the 'essential nature of the performance' thereunder so as to constitute 'commercial impracticability.'"[377]

---

[375] Casebook p. 772.
[376] Casebook p. 772.
[377] Casebook p. 792.

## 8.3 Problems of Performance

### 8.3.1 The Obligation to Perform in Good Faith

#### 8.3.1.1 Duty to Avoid Interfering with Performance: *Patterson v. Meyerhofer*

1. Meyerhofer agreed to buy four properties from Patterson, which he planned to buy at an auction. Meyerhofer ended up bidding for the same properties in the same auction, winning them for $620 less than she would have paid Patterson.

2. The court held for Patterson. "In the case of every contract there is an implied undertaking on the part of each party that he will not intentionally and purposely do anything to prevent the other party from carrying out the agreement on his part."[378]

#### 8.3.1.2 Indirect Interference: *Iron Trade Products Co. v. Wilkoff Co.*

1. The plaintiff contracted with the defendant to buy 2,600 tons of relaying rails. Afterward, the plaintiff bought 887 tons of similar rails on the open market. Rails were scarce, so the plaintiff's second purchase caused the defendant to be unable to find rails to fill its obligation except at exorbitant prices, rendering performance impossible.

2. The court held for the plaintiff, finding that "[m]ere difficulty of performance will not excuse a breach of contract."[379]

#### 8.3.1.3 *Kirke La Shelle Co. v. Paul Armstrong Co.*

1. " . . . in every contract there exists an implied covenant of good faith and fair dealing."[380]

#### 8.3.1.4 The UCC Definitions of Good Faith

1. Good faith in the UCC means "honesty in fact and the observance of reasonable commercial standards of fair dealing."[381]

#### 8.3.1.5 Duty to Perform in Good Faith under the UCC and Restatement Second

1. Both the UCC and the Restatement (Second) require good faith performance.

---

[378]Casebook p. 887.
[379]Casebook p. 889.
[380]Casebook p. 890.
[381]Casebook p. 891.

### 8.3.1.6 Farnsworth, "Good Faith in Contract Performance"

1. What does "good faith" mean?[382]

    (a) Farnsworth: it's a fundamental idea of contract law. It implies terms in the contract.

    (b) Summers: the "excluder" analysis asks, what does a judge want to rule out by use of the phrase "good faith"? It has no meaning on its own, but it serves to exclude many heterogeneous forms of bad faith.

    (c) Burton: the "forgone opportunity analysis" argues that "good faith" limits what a party can do in performance, so bad faith is to "recapture opportunities forgone upon contracting . . . "

    (d) Courts apply all three standards.

---

[382] Casebook pp. 892–93.

www.ingramcontent.com/pod-product-compliance
Lightning Source LLC
Chambersburg PA
CBHW062215220526
45471CB00009B/3214